Tom Kite is the 1992 U.S. Open champion and the all-time leading money winner on the PGA Tour.

STEP THREE: Three-Quarter Backswing

STEP FOUR: Backswing Completed

THE
EIGHT-STEP
SWING

ALSO BY JIM MCLEAN
GOLF DIGEST'S BOOK OF DRILLS

THIS BOOK IS DEDICATED TO MY FAMILY:
JUSTINE, MATT, AND JON.

*My wife, Justine, has supported my efforts
and stood by me as I traveled, studied, and
moved forward in my career as a golf instructor.*

*My boys, Matt and Jon, are the light of my life—
by far the greatest thing ever to happen to me.
I love you all.*

THE EIGHT-STEP SWING

A REVOLUTIONARY GOLF TECHNIQUE BY A PRO COACH

FOREWORD BY TOM KITE

JIM McLEAN

ILLUSTRATIONS BY DOM LUPO
PHOTOGRAPHS BY JEFF BLANTON

HarperCollins*Publishers*

HarperCollins books may be purchased for educational, business,
or sales promotional use. For information please write:
Special Markets Department, HarperCollins Publishers, Inc.,
10 East 53rd Street, New York, NY 10022.

FIRST EDITION

Designed by Joel Avirom and Jason Snyder
Illustrations copyright © 1994 by Dom Lupo
Photographs copyright ©1994 by Jeff Blanton

Library of Congress Cataloging-in-Publication Data

McLean, Jim.
    The eight-step swing : a revolutionary golf technique by a
pro coach / Jim McLean. — 1st ed.
      p.   cm.
    Includes index.
    ISBN 0-06-017073-5
    1. Swing (Golf). I. Title.
GV979.S9M32   1994
796.352'3—dc20   93-39839

---

94 95 96 97 98 ❖/RRD 10 9 8 7 6 5 4 3 2

CONTENTS

FOREWORD

I cannot think of a more qualified person to be writing a book on advanced quality golf instruction than Jim McLean. I realize that this statement may surprise you somewhat, with the vast numbers of golf instructors out there pushing their methods and ideals. Yes, there are some who have spent more time on the practice tee with students. That may just be because they are older or because they do not have a "club job" and need report only to their students. But time certainly cannot be the determining measure of how good a teacher is. It must be the knowledge acquired and the ability to communicate it to the student.

In my opinion, Jim has earned the right to author this book. Why? Plainly and simply, he has the knowledge. Jim has gone the extra mile to talk to the top players and teachers and pick their brains for any tidbit of information that may help him become first a better player and then a better teacher. Jackie Burke, Gary Player, Harvey Penick, Paul Runyan, Ben Hogan, Bob Charles, Ben Crenshaw, Don January, Byron Nelson, and even I, are only a few of those who have been quizzed by Jim.

But how one handles that knowledge has to be just as important. Jim has seen that there is not only one way to play the game and, therefore, there cannot be only one method to teach it. An experienced teacher knows he or she must take what the student has and work within those limitations. After all, we are all human and all different. Jim McLean cannot be categorized as a "method" teacher. Sure, he has fundamentals that support his teaching—fundamentals that are well supported by those players listed above. But he is not a "do it my way or else" kind of guy.

Jim has proven that with knowledge and versatility he can help students with a range of handicaps—everyone from the rank beginner to the veteran PGA Tour professional. This book will prove he also can help teachers improve their methods.

Tom Kite

ACKNOWLEDGMENTS

This is an important page for me personally. This book began several years ago, growing out of notes and ideas I had compiled, lessons I took, and what I learned from watching top instructors coach golf. My notes and ideas expanded to overwhelming numbers, until finally I found the time to organize them into some semblance of order. However, it took the efforts of a good friend of mine, Dave Collins, to take all of my material and type it into a computer. That was back in 1989. The original book was huge and was to be called *The Total Package*, because it encompassed all aspects of golf.

When I later decided to trim that original book and create this one, with its central point being the "Eight Steps," I called again on the services of Dave Collins. I am grateful to him for his constructive comments and the many hours he devoted to this book in its initial stages.

After Dave came a professional writer, Dave Gould, who faced the incredible tasks of organizing and editing. I owe him thanks, too, for putting up with my deletions and rewrites. I'm sure it was extremely frustrating. Thanks, Dave.

Next, my friend John Andrisani, the senior instruction editor of *Golf Magazine*, reedited and reorganized the script and coordinated the artwork with Dom Lupo and the photographs with Jeff Blanton. John is a real pro who has been through this process many times. I'm grateful for his expert opinions and service.

Last, I must thank my former great staff at Sleepy Hollow Country Club, who all participated in some way with this effort, especially my entire teaching staff.

Few club professionals have been as fortunate as I. The members of Sleepy Hollow and the staff at Doral allowed me tremendous freedom to work and grow as an instructor. While I've given outside lessons to pros and amateurs and traveled during the season to teach at tournament sites or to conduct out-of-town seminars, they stood by me. Thank you Sleepy Hollow; we are friends for life. Thank you, Doral.

INTRODUCTION

Back in 1975, I decided to learn everything possible about how the game of golf is played and how it should be taught. Having set myself a goal of becoming an outstanding teacher, I made a series of commitments. One of them was to write regularly in a journal devoted to the golf swing. Whenever I came across a new idea or a new discovery I would at least scribble it on paper. Then, when the golf shop and the lesson schedule quieted down, I could go back and fill in the blanks.

Before very long, the writing difficulties I expected to have were replaced by an opposite problem: I couldn't stop. I couldn't stop writing because everywhere I went there was new information or new evidence relating to old information or just new, creative ways of communicating the time-honored principles.

Of course, I have to say, I went to a lot of the right places. My model for teaching golf and the golf swing comes from those sources, including watching Sam Snead in tournament play a dozen times and on videotape thousands of times. I saw Ben Hogan's swing in person over the course of a half dozen rounds and several practice sessions as well as on videotape maybe ten thousand times. I watched and spoke with Roberto de Vicenzo whenever I could. I played more than one hundred rounds of golf with Ken Venturi and seemed to learn something significant from him every round. I've been able to play in tournaments with Bruce Lietzke, John Mahaffey, Bill Rogers, Ben Crenshaw, Johnny Miller, Tom Kite, Lanny Wadkins, Payne Stewart, Fuzzy Zoeller, Gil Morgan, and many other top competitors.

In Texas, at the Champions Golf Club, I played with Jackie Burke and watched Jimmy Demaret practice his game. Later I conducted golf schools with Jackie in New York. I also learned a lot about what it takes to be a champion by spending time with Gary Player on the practice tee. Gardner Dickinson helped me tremendously. I observed and took lessons from Bob Toski and went out on the golf course with him. I've taught at numerous golf schools and golf workshops with the leading sports psychologists: Bob Rotella, David Cook, Dick Coop, Chuck Hogan, and Fran Pirozzolo. I've taken golf lessons from Johnny Revolta, Jack Grout, Jim Flick, Toney Penna, Jimmy Ballard, David Leadbetter, John Elliott, Homer Kelley, Gary McCord, Ben Doyle, Claude Harmon, Dick and Craig Harmon (Claude's sons), Gene Sarazen, Joe Nichols, Carl Lohren, Harry Cooper, Bob Watson, John Geertsen, Vinny Grillo, and many others.

I believe I have read practically everything written in the English language about golf.

I got my start as a golf instructor from one of the best swingers I have ever seen and one of the best golfers I've ever played with: Al Mengert. Mengert played in nine U.S. Opens and ten PGA championships, and played the Tour for many years. He worked under Claude Harmon at Winged Foot and Tommy Armour at Boca Raton. Al took me under his wing and encouraged me tremendously as a player, a teacher, and a club professional.

Perhaps my best piece of luck was to have Carl Welty working as an assistant pro at a nine-hole golf club not far from the neighborhood where I was raised. This was in Seattle, Washington, in 1966, and Carl already had amassed a great collection of golf swings on film—eight and sixteen millimeter. Carl showed me the dynamic movements of the swing in a way that is possible only with slow-motion film. He pointed out facets and subtleties that were not talked about or written about at all back then.

Since those early days, Carl has continued to collect films and videotapes of golf swings at an amazing rate. Nobody I have met in golf comes close to having studied golf swings the way Carl has. Almost a "mad scientist" of the golf swing, Carl has devoted hour after hour, day after day, year after year to the study of great players' swings. Through his film and tape library, which is unparalleled, he has given me the basis for my swing model and my teaching method. In the golf profession, to say that you teach the fundamentals and dynamics that characterize the greatest players' swings is just a beginning. *You have to know exactly what those characteristics are*—what is absolute and what is an allowable deviation. Working cooperatively with Carl, I have been able to learn this information cold.

Through the years, our procedure has been a simple one. I would travel around the country seeking out the most respected teachers and learn from them their concept of what happens in the swing. Then I would bring these ideas back to Carl's screening room and together we would put them to "the test." For the concepts I had gathered in my field research to be valid, the Welty films and tapes would have to show that the swings of Ben Hogan, Byron Nelson, Sam Snead, Arnold Palmer, Gary Player, Jack Nicklaus, Lee Trevino, Tom Watson, Gene

Littler, Roberto de Vicenzo, Calvin Peete, Seve Ballesteros, and Nick Faldo embodied them.

The Jim McLean *Eight-Step Swing* system is a consolidation of all I have seen and heard in my long study of what has worked for the great players and not worked for the not-so-greats. In presenting it, I always strive to be organized and specific. I learned the importance of this from working with Jimmy Ballard beginning in 1977 in Pell City, Alabama. What organization! Ballard worked from an unchanging set of seven common denominators, and he had his method down pat. I paid to go through his golf school nine times, and I later watched him for many hours in his work with top tour players and average amateur golfers. Ballard, of all instructors, exemplified to me the principle of organization and a systemized approach to helping people improve.

By the early 1980s, I felt prepared to write out my ideas on the golf swing in a formal way. In the mid-1980s I began to speak at teaching and playing workshops of the PGA of America all around the country. This experience forced me to become even more disciplined and organized in my thinking and presentation.

Using videotape every day in every lesson and conferring with Carl Welty on an ongoing basis, I eventually came up with eight key checkpoint positions for the swing. Really, they are eight video checkpoint steps along the way to a fundamentally sound golf swing. Each step offers an *ideal* plus some *leeway*. There are not eight exact positions you must achieve. To fit yourself into the swing patterns of all the greats requires allowances for your own personal differences. To represent this, I came up with the concept of *Corridors of Success*. These are parameters within which I like to see any swing fall. Body motions or swing movements that fall outside these corridors usually need to be changed. A student who exceeds the leeway margins of my eight steps would have trouble, I contend, hitting good shots consistently.

In fact, serious violations at certain points of the swing deserve to be called, in my terminology, *Death Moves*. A *Death Move* is an action or position that is so far from ideal that it will cause you to hit poor shots forever. With a violation of golf swing fundamentals that is this dramatic, I recommend an immediate change.

The road to consistent quality in your golf swing is a difficult one, but you can take heart in the fact that professional instruction focuses on elimination, not addition. In my day-to-day teaching, I am most often cleaning up and simplifying a movement or body action. Typically, a student's swing is worked with to make it less complicated, rather than more complicated. Simplicity and repetition—these are beautiful goals to have in your golf-improvement program.

Finally, let me state what would appear at first to be a contradiction. I teach beginners much differently from the way I teach advanced players. In fact, I teach a totally different concept to each group. My instruction for novices revolves around the hands and arms. Conversely, I teach the advanced player to focus on body control, with an absence of hand action. In both cases, however, the goal is the same: to move your swing inside the *Corridors of Success* that are laid out in *The Eight-Step Swing*.

Jim McLean

THE
EIGHT-STEP
SWING

THE RIGHT MIND-SET
CONFUSION CAN OPEN THE DOOR TO DISCOVERY

Improving your golf game is a mental, physical—some would say spiritual—quest. It's a wonderful, worthy endeavor, but it comes a lot easier to someone who can handle momentary confusion. You see, in golf, confusion is sometimes *necessary*. Rather than something to avoid, confusion in the learning process is actually something to welcome. Confusion indicates to me that a student is truly thinking or feeling in a new way.

In plain fact, any time you take a formal lesson from a professional, try a tip from a golf magazine, or attempt to change your golf game in any way, you're likely to become confused. Whatever the change, be it a theory or a drill or an idea, it should result in a new "feel." This change in feel, this departure from your normal technique, is what triggers mental confusion. But confusion is a good thing and a very normal part of the learning process. In fact, *confusion opens the door to discovering new ways to swing and play better golf.*

The best way to handle confusion is to see past it, to the new understanding that awaits you. As you work through your confused state of mind (and body), you should welcome feeling new sensations involved in the swing, even though you aren't quite sure where each one will take you. If, in the end, these new elements of change don't feel good or fail to help you swing better, you can always go back to where you were before, knowing at the very least that *you gained by learning what doesn't work for you.*

The alternatives to the improvement quest are giving up completely on new thoughts or, worse, deciding that you know it all. In either case, you stop learning. By quitting, you admit that either you've "got it" or you never had all the answers and that you are satisfied with the golf skills you presently possess. No problem with this, except that I find most human beings are naturally curious and do possess an inner desire to excel. Some people will resist all change, yet we know change is the only thing that brings about progress for someone making fundamental mistakes. Hard work and repetition of the same old wrong techniques is *not* the path to mastery.

The swing is vastly complex, and there are many ways to attain excellent results. There are many paths that can be taken and many that will allow you to reach a satisfactory destination. However, now is a good time to sound a warning: *An abundance of what is written on the golf swing is controversial and contradicts other expert views, point by point. Mixing ideas from totally different concepts can be frustrating and is usually counterproductive.*

Confusion can be removed from the process only in one case: when a pure "method" teacher meets a student who believes *completely* in the method being taught and is physically adaptable to it. At that point, the golfer becomes a disciple. He or she accepts absolute statements about the golf swing the way zealots accept their religious tenets. The human mind is so strong that total belief in a teacher's method literally makes things happen. Thus the student reaches a high level of mental clarity and focus. If the method is sound, the result: an average golfer becomes good; a good golfer becomes great.

Having said this, I'm truly convinced that the best method in the world cannot suit every golfer or even most golfers. The game and the swing are too individualized to allow for a series of absolutes. As I see it, there can be no unquestionably "correct way" to teach every player. Pure "method instructors" who become confident that they have seen it all and learned it all have probably just stopped noticing new things and have begun looking only for what they want to see. Students who never experience even a moment of confusion are either vastly brilliant or close-minded.

On the driving range, most of you have experienced that

odd feeling of hitting virtually every shot exactly as you want, to the point that you decide to experiment. You ask yourself, "Can I switch to a different swing action or swing thought and still get excellent results?" or "Now that I'm hitting the ball on the exact line as planned, can I stretch out the shot and get better distance?" Often, of course, this questioning process breaks your good swing and shot-making spell, but I wouldn't be too quick to criticize you for being inquisitive. Golf is such a demanding quest, we are often unable to discontinue searching, even when our goals are temporarily reached. We all tend to want just a little bit more.

Ironically, when you have something that works, it is not a sure indication that this is the only answer. It doesn't mean that another approach will not work or that trying a new approach won't produce better results or a more interesting experience. However, be careful not to become too much of a technical perfectionist, or you'll experiment forever. Seek to *crystallize* your concept of what you are doing, bearing in mind that the key points within that concept will change and develop and, one hopes, improve your game even more.

I tell some of my students it may actually be better for them to accentuate their uniqueness, rather than try to swing like everyone else. Difference is one definition of greatness, is it not? Great athletes all use divergent ideas and techniques to perform at their peak levels. Consider, for example, the varying techniques of Ben Hogan, Jack Nicklaus, Lee Trevino, Fred Couples, Corey Pavin, Ray Floyd, Lanny Wadkins, John Daly, Bruce Lietzke, and Curtis Strange.

At this juncture, let me insert an important reminder: *Please don't make the mistake of becoming overly serious in your quest. You'll be sure of getting in your own way if you turn golf into a somber, laborious exercise. Avoid self-importance and excessive self-criticism. Improvement comes much faster to the person who has fun and plays for the love of the game. The childlike learner who appreciates the beauty of the game and the thrill of discovery will get the most that golf has to give.*

Belief in yourself is the key ingredient to greatness. "Belief is durable" the saying goes, and in golf that means trusting

The varying techniques of Ben Hogan (left), Jack Nicklaus (center), and John Daly (right) prove that there is no "one" perfect way to swing.

your system, your swing method, and your style of play. It is either difficult or impossible to alter a person's deeper beliefs; this is a simple fact. Over time, however, beliefs can change. For example, some of my teenage thoughts about the golf swing now seem ridiculous to me. I remember that when my boys were three and four years old, they believed with all of their hearts that a monster lived in the closet. My point: believing does not, in the end, make something true. But remember, beliefs are very powerful.

Another axiom holds: "It is better to travel hopefully than to arrive." But sometimes we do arrive. If, in your quest, you have used a drill to work toward a certain feeling and result and you get that result, it's time to put aside the drill. Come back to the drill if the fundamentals it has helped you refine begin to break down, but know when to stop.

The bottom line is that only one person can make you great. That person is you, not some teacher. Teachers, books, and methods can only provide limited assistance and guidance. You alone must do the work and pay the price through hard, honest practice. You alone must be able to withstand pressure and hit the shots on the most solitary stage of all—the golf course.

The quest is similar from golfer to golfer, but there are many paths to choose from. *Doing it one's own way (with or without an instructor's help) produces the greatness of champions.* To believe in yourself is to have power; whereas conforming to the current norms will almost always create mediocrity, leaving you just short of your personal best and far short of brilliance. Only you can make the choice as to what physical skills and drills you will use to become a total player. The interesting outcome of it all is that, at a certain advanced stage of play, the game of golf becomes almost totally *mental.*

How to Prepare
Establishing a Good Battle Plan Is Bound to Raise Your Level of Play in Tournaments

"The general who wins a battle makes many calculations in his temple before the battle is fought."

—Sun Tzu,
The Art of War

Golfers who like to compete do not like to approach a tournament without being fully prepared. But, honestly, what percentage of the time can you expect to bring your A game into competition? Usually there is some facet, maybe your driver, your putter, or your short-iron game, that is not at its sharpest.

If that's the bad news, then the good news is this: no matter how well or poorly you are playing, no matter what your realistic chances are of winning the tournament, you can *always* win what I call the "four battles." By being totally prepared in these four areas, you will be at your best for any important event you enter.

Credit for this proven concept of establishing a competitive golf "battle plan" goes to Coach Jim Young and the Performance Institute of the Academy at West Point. He told me that there were five contests within every game that his Army varsity football team could win. Let me explain. The Army team applied a basic game plan to each contest it played. The idea was that even if Army was playing number-one-ranked Notre Dame the team could still win individual aspects of the game, which could, in the end, lead to victory or at least a highly competitive game. I wondered if I could apply this same thinking to golf. Eventually, I came up with the following four-point battle plan, designed to help you perform more proficiently under pressure.

BATTLE NUMBER ONE

W I N THE PRETOURNAMENT BATTLE. To win the pretournament battle, you must begin your preparation for the tournament well in advance. Finish up projects that have been hanging. Get to all those long, important phone calls to business associates and family. Go to the eye doctor, the dentist, the chiropractor. Then begin your homework on the golf course you'll be playing. Even if you've played it many times, walk it with a notepad and pencil. Determine where you want to hit the ball, then locate the "bailout" spots where you wouldn't mind seeing your mishit shots land. Where there's a layup shot facing you, plan that layup shot down to the last little bounce, making sure to land the ball a specific distance from the pin. Be sure you know exactly how far you are hitting your wedges that day. Finally, carefully analyze your golf game. Determine what area of your game needs the most work and get to it. (Always spend some extra time before any event working on putting and chipping.) The object is to begin all your tournament preparations well in advance.

BATTLE NUMBER TWO

WIN THE PREROUND BATTLE. Start by getting your equipment in perfect order. Make sure every grip is clean and tacky; every groove on every iron is scraped clean; your golf balls are marked for identification; your shoes are respiked; and you've got extra gloves, sweater, sunscreen, lip balm, water jug, lucky socks, and whatever you could possibly think of later and say, "I wish I'd brought my . . . "

Then, every day of the event, block out an excessively long space of time between your departure for the course and your tee time. Know exactly how long it takes to get to the golf course and then give yourself twice that amount of time. I remember the first time I saw Lee Trevino in the locker room at Sleepy Hollow Country Club, in Scarborough, New York, several hours before his tee time for the PGA Senior Tour Commemorative. I asked him why he was so early, and he explained to me his routine—the point of which is to leave nothing to chance and to remove completely the possibility of feeling rushed. If Trevino hits traffic, needs gas, has a flat tire, takes a wrong turn, he never has to worry, because he factors these long-shot possibilities into his schedule. Trevino can always be found in the locker room well before his scheduled tee time in a tournament, doing what some people would call wasting time. True, he is talking, resting, or just hanging out—but he's not wasting time. He's preparing to win a golf tournament, and he knows that to play his best he has to have some down time among all the essentials of travel, getting dressed, eating, and hitting practice shots. By arriving extra early, Lee knows he will walk out of that locker room for his preround practice exactly on time. He will be ready to focus and he will never be rushed.

You *can't* control how the wind blows, so concentrate on the things you can control, one of which is remembering to check the wind direction before teeing off and to anticipate how and which way it will be blowing on every hole. Usually, there is a flag near the clubhouse that will help this determination. Remember that on the course the wind may be swirling through different areas and can fool you if you are not truly aware of the general direction.

Go through your warmup routine in exactly the way it makes you feel most comfortable. I recommend putting first and then going to the driving range to warm up the full swing. I feel that those warmup putts are quite important (especially some long lag putts) to establish the green speed and your "feel" for the day.

Lee Trevino's practice sessions are a vital part of his preround battle plan.

Finish your warmup session using the club you will hit off the first tee. Rehearse that shot in detail and you will feel much more relaxed heading to the first tee. Allow extra time to reach the tee. This will allow you to focus and prepare for your all-important first tee shot of the day.

BATTLE NUMBER THREE

WIN THE EMOTIONAL BATTLE. Entire books are written about the emotional and mental approach to sports, including golf. You should know the mental/emotional state that allows you to perform at your best. The one tip I would add is this: before you tee off, it is often helpful to realize that every round usually has bogeys in it. The thing is, we don't know where, when, or if they will come. Many fine rounds have early bogeys, sometimes two in a row. Promise yourself that if you bogey hole one and hole two, you will visualize your scorecard with those bogeys isolated among a long string of pars. Remember, that scoring bogeys on holes number one and two is not a sure sign of your worst round. On the other hand, if you start out with two birdies, the reverse is true. It does not mean you should do anything different. Stick to your game plan and do not project results. Continue your shot-by-shot mentality. Stay in the present tense. Accept your success without taking on any doubts or unreal responsibilities to shoot a record score.

Winning the emotional battle will be more difficult on certain days. However, this remains a battle that you are capable of winning every time, provided you maintain your composure, even when you swing poorly or don't score to the best of your abilities on a particular hole or several holes.

Anger usually brings mistakes that add strokes to your score. Needless risks are then taken, and your score gets worse. That is why it's extremely important to stay mentally level and focused. Sure, I know it's easy to get upset in golf. The irony is, in some cases that anger can be helpful in snapping you out of a funk. However, if you go into each round knowing that luck is involved and that every shot you hit will not be your best, then attitude problems can be greatly reduced.

I find it very useful to have students keep things in perspective. We would all do well to play golf shot by shot or hole by hole, and leave each hole behind as we move to the next. So many of us play golf in the past or in the future, when we really need to play in the present.

Jackie Burke always told the University of Houston golf team to focus on the performance at hand and to forget about results. Burke taught me a number of vital lessons about golf during my college days, but none was more important than his two-sided formula of $P/R = \$$, whereas $R/P = 0$. Translation: *performance over results leads to success, whereas emphasizing results over performance leads to failure.*

It's okay to form a result-oriented goal. But if you are result conscious while you are performing, if you think ahead while there are shots still to be hit, you may not be able to take care of the shot at hand. Your mind will be distracted from the present and your performance will not be 100 percent. Living in the future or the past is not the optimal performance state. It is a distraction. Take care of the shot at hand and those coveted good results will happen. *Performance first—always.*

BATTLE NUMBER FOUR

WIN THE MANAGEMENT BATTLE. Before you tee off, eat and drink what you need to avoid mental or physical fatigue. Then once you begin your round, you will stay mentally connected to the golf course and how it's playing, especially in regard to wind, moisture, dryness, mowing, watering, etc. Promise yourself that you won't get caught on a tee without the right club, because you let the caddie walk ahead or you parked the cart too far away. Promise yourself that you will follow a set "game plan" that involves not taking unrealistic risks. Between shots, relax and pace yourself. Do not try to concentrate intensely for the full duration of the round.

Winning the management battle requires that you fairly assess your strengths and weaknesses and then maximize your strengths. Good course managers do not make dumb mistakes. They are aware of everything and miss nothing. They can "zone out" distractions. They plan and "see" each shot.

Golf is a game of adjustments, and usually the player who makes the fewest and the least costly mistakes will remain in the game with a good chance to win. Whatever physical mistakes you commit in competition, you should be able to contain them and move on if your preparation is thorough and if you make sure to control everything that's controllable.

I believe that it's possible for you to win all four of these battles. Try, and you will give yourself the best opportunity to compete at your optimum level, time and time again.

Body Motions for Advanced Golf
A Clear Understanding of the Pivot Actions Involved in the Backswing and Downswing Is a Vital Prerequisite to Hitting the Ball Powerfully and Accurately

My usual approach to working with *intermediate to advanced* players is to make sure that they mentally understand, and physically feel, the basic elements of the backswing and downswing *pivot* actions. These actions, involving particularly the feet, knees, hips, shoulders, and head, comprise the nucleus of the swing in that they allow a player to move the club back properly to the top and then deliver it squarely and powerfully into the back of the ball, without any conscious manipulation of the hands being necessary. Essentially, the pivot is what allows the entire swing motion to operate virtually on *automatic pilot*. For this reason, I will now describe and break down the vital elements of the pivot in the simplest possible manner. Understanding them will expedite the learning process and ready you for the more sophisticated steps of the swing, which will be presented in Chapter 7.

THE BACKSWING PIVOT

ELEMENT ONE: FOOTWORK

Tremendous emphasis is placed on your connection to the club—your grip—but what about your grip on the ground? Think about it: much of the power you apply to the golf ball

Good footwork and solid weight shift on the backswing promote an athletic golf swing.

traces itself back to the resistance point between your feet and the ground. Good footwork is necessary in all sports and certainly to the execution of an effective golf swing. When your footwork is right, your lower body resistance is sound as well.

Good footwork is athletic in appearance throughout the swing. It is lively, efficient, and powerful. During the setup, the weight is equally balanced on your feet. However, it should never favor being forward toward the toes. If anything, the weight is more toward the heels than the toes. As the back-swing starts, there is first a feeling of slight weight shift off the inside of the left instep, with a constant increase of weight shift to the inside of the right foot (*toward the right heel*) and right

Poor footwork usually runs toward either of two extremes:

1. An absence of foot-work—golfer glued to the ground.

2. The golfer's left heel lifts early, with the weight too far forward.

The "flat foot" plants all twenty-two spikes in the ground and doesn't let go, causing the arms to flail away at the ball. The "tap dancer" is up on the toes of the left foot early in the backswing, causing a lower body sway or overrotation of the knees.

Check carefully for foot faults.

leg. I like to see the weight shift occur early as the club head travels away from the target.

It is fine, on long shots, for the left heel to come off the ground during a full backswing if it is *pulled* off the ground by the force of your weight shift and pivot. It is not fine for the left heel to be lifted off the ground voluntarily, as an unconnected act. If it does rise, and I think it can on long shots, the left heel should never go more than a few inches off the ground. Many top players keep the left heel on the ground even for a full drive.

ELEMENT TWO: KNEE ACTION

Your knee action and knee turn will, to a large degree, dictate the amount of hip rotation you ultimately make. Freeze your knees, and your hips will be "frozen" as well—they *can't* pivot!

Controlled knee action is a key to both resistance and rotation.

If you employ too much knee action or knee turn, your hips will be free to overrotate. There will be no lower body resistance, thus you will have great difficulty returning to proper impact alignments. (Exaggerated knee action is very common among high handicap golfers.)

Proper knee motion involves both knees. On the backswing, the left knee breaks inward and outward simultaneously. It simply stays in sync with the total release of the entire left side in your take-away. The danger occurs when the left knee travels too far in either direction. Too much left knee movement causes slack in the legs and often results in a lower body slide. Don't allow the left knee to pass your spine or your centerline. (The modern golf backswing action is usually characterized by "quiet" knee and leg action.)

The right knee action is critical to the bracing of the entire right leg and hip. The right knee does not freeze, but it's a plus if you can maintain your flex throughout the backswing. The *Death Move* for the right knee is sliding (not straightening). When the right knee slides, your weight will move incorrectly to the outside of the right leg and your lower body resistance will diminish greatly. So, in effect, you "post up" against the braced right knee in a solid backswing.

ELEMENT THREE: HIP ACTION

The lower body should resist the turning of the upper body during the backswing (to create torque), then initiate the downswing by releasing that torque. Think of it as a spring being wound in your hips and torso, then unwound with a torquing power that accelerates the shoulders, arms, and club. Less hip movement on the backswing usually translates into a more powerful movement on the forward swing.

I must caution you that resistance in the hips can be overdone. When the knees freeze, the hips cannot turn. So the knees must rotate some to allow the hips to rotate. I routinely see students who need more hip turn. Either they lack rotation of the knees or they slide the knees and hips back. There must be some turn over the right leg. The right hip must go back around. The *Corridor of Success* ranges from approximately

Top players realize that hip action is a vital link to power.

forty to forty-five degrees of hip turn for the very supple player to sixty to sixty-five for the less flexible who cannot make a full shoulder turn without the extra hip rotation. It is just a fact that I see far more students who overturn and overwork the knees and the hips on the backswing than do it correctly. Thus lower body resistance is usually a great thought to have in mind if you want to pivot correctly and, in turn, increase both your power and your accuracy.

ELEMENT FOUR: SHOULDER MOVEMENT

The shoulders make the biggest turn in the backswing. It's often useful to visualize the shoulders turning twice as much as the hips. On a full driver swing, you might see your critical body motions in the following terms: the knees turn twenty-five degrees and the hips fifty degrees, while the shoulders turn one hundred degrees.

The shoulders turn on an axis. Again, it is useful to see your shoulders rotating on their own plane. Your "spine angle" at address determines the shoulder axis.

The shoulders must not turn level like a merry-go-round, which will bring the arms and club too far inside and around. Conversely, they must not overtilt like a Ferris wheel, which causes the swing to be too vertical.

When you correctly turn your shoulders, you will feel as if your right shoulder were going up and behind your head, while your left shoulder traveled level and behind the ball.

It's very possible to overturn the shoulders. On all but the fullest swing, the shoulders will not turn more than ninety degrees. *It is the gap between the shoulders and hips that creates the torque in the body. Therefore, the largest percentage of turn must come from the shoulders.*

When the shoulders overturn, the arms are carried too far and eventually weight begins to "tip over" into the left side. Overrotating the shoulders thus can cause a reverse pivot. The overturn causes a host of other problems, including pulling the head and eyes off the ball and loss of balance. Golfers with this problem need to limit the amount of rotation in the shoulders to gain more power.

ELEMENT FIVE: HEAD MOVEMENT

The head turns and/or moves to the right slightly. It has to, or the pivot will be so tense and mechanical that you will not employ a free, athletic backswing action. In a full swing, a top player rotates the chin to the right twenty to twenty-five degrees. Harvey Penick, the famous teacher, probably put it best: "Show me a player who doesn't move his head, and I'll show you someone who can't play."

Although head movement is a necessary part of the pivot, for best results your eyes should remain focused on the ball. It's the pivot and movement of the head that allow you to make

Natural head rotation allows for a powerful windup.

a complete shoulder turn, while freezing the head into a stationary post hinders the turning action of the shoulders, robbing you of vital power. The turn or rotation of the head means there are four specific turns that I look at in the golf swing.

THE DOWNSWING PIVOT

ELEMENT ONE: FOOTWORK

During the downswing, the weight shifts from the right post to the left post, off the inside of the right foot. This is crucial to employing the two-pivot-point swing.

The correct right foot and right heel movements reveal what is occurring with the golfer's weight shift and hip action. In most ways, the right heel only "reacts" to the body center. As the hips hit the forward wall of lateral shift, there's an abrupt stop. The left leg has firmed and resisted the lateral motion. The hips are in the process of "raising" through impact, and by impact they have also opened to the target. In effect, the turning hips and body center pull the right heel up. This causes a microsecond stop and/or quiver of the right foot. I've never heard anyone mention or write about it, but it definitely does occur during the swings of many of the game's best golfers.

Many great players, in particular Sam Snead, have used the "push off the right foot" as a tremendous swing key. The right heel kicks forward and toward the ball. On full shots the right heel is off the ground at impact, and the right foot continues to lift until only the toe is touching the ground. I have found it most interesting that many of the all-time greats slide their right foot forward and that their right heel moves up before impact, then moves downward, then back up. This is a clear indication of forward drive, before the player hits the braced-up "wall" of the body's left side. A common thought that many powerful ball hitters use to initiate the downswing is "Replant the left heel."

Good footwork on the downswing helps put the club in the perfect delivery position.

Death Move: a common fault of poor footwork is for the left heel to back up on the forward swing. When I see this, I know that the golfer has "spun out." Because the left hip and left heel must work in the same direction, I know that the golfer has spun his or her left hip back.

ELEMENT TWO: KNEE ACTION

The typical amateur has too much knee action in the backswing and too little in the downswing. In contrast, the typical tour

On the downswing, the knees first shift, then rotate.

professional resists with the lower body, then really uses the ground and the knees to pump forward into the finish.

It doesn't matter which knee triggers the downswing. What's important is that both knees move laterally, then rotate, and at the finish of the swing, virtually touch one another. (In some great swings, the left knee noticeably leads the downswing. However, this move can be overdone, causing an excessive slide.) See page 86: The Sit Down.

ELEMENT THREE: HIP ACTION

As the right knee moves outward toward the ball, the hips recenter and the right heel raises ever so slightly. Then, as the body's "center" rises through impact and the hips rotate diago-

Hips and triangle rotating in unison.

nally left, the right heel hesitates or drops down slightly. This unique and very brisk up-and-down movement of the right heel is at least partially triggered by the right knee changing direction and moving the way of the rotating hips. It is an interesting observation, but not something you should think about.

As the body fully releases and the player's weight is fully forward, the hips actually turn left of the target. Finally, the player is balanced on his or her right toe, with the knees together and no space at all between the thighs.

On the downswing, the hips slide between seven and twelve inches toward the target in combination with a forceful and powerful hip rotation. Unquestionably, there is *lateral motion*.

Even though the hips lead the shoulders, the more quickly

A final important thought regarding the shoulders is that their motion must be uninterrupted, with no stops or delays at or past impact. Feel the left shoulder continue to rotate left and backward through the ball.

Watch the head movement of a top player during his or her swing. Notice that the chin rotates to the right on the backswing, reenters the address position for a freeze-frame at impact, then rotates toward the target at the finish. As it is pivoting, it may also move laterally—to the right during the backswing and to the left during the forward swing. Like the body as a whole, the head pivots and also moves in creating a powerful swing and shot. The head has a pivot and it moves slightly right and then left to create enough freedom for the shoulders to make a powerful coil.

The head has its own "miniature swing."

rotating shoulders are able, in effect, nearly to catch up to the hips at impact. Both hips and shoulders are open to the target line at impact, with the hips still ahead and still more open. Make no mistake, however, it's the hips or lower body that lead the parade and provide the initiation of power in the swing.

ELEMENT FOUR: SHOULDER MOVEMENT

The shoulders must not actually initiate the downswing. The stored energy in the upper torso (created by the gap between the hips and shoulders) plus the work of the lower body will cause the shoulders to unwind with tremendous force. However, the golfer must wait that split second for the lower body to begin the motion. When this occurs, the right shoulder will first lower and then rotate around and forward.

The spine will naturally lean slightly away from the target—slightly more than at the address position. This will be a totally natural occurrence, due completely to the proper sequencing of body motion. It is never something to think about while playing, because it will almost always cause other problems. Rather, the golfer should focus on having the shoulders respond to the lower body. Good footwork causes the shoulders to work correctly.

I have observed that many players tend to lower the right shoulder dramatically; this causes the spine to lean too far back at impact and also promotes an inside-out swing motion. A good swing thought for you is to think *level* on the forward swing with the shoulders. This thought encourages the shoulders to rotate "on plane," or perfectly on their axis.

As the swing is completed, the shoulders will brake and reflex back to a target-facing position. This is a beautifully controlled movement.

ELEMENT FIVE: HEAD MOVEMENT

Around twenty years ago, Johnny Miller (who is an avid student of the swing) made an offhand comment to me about the head pivoting and having its own swinging motion. I really liked that image and have used it in my teaching ever since. The head has its own miniature swing.

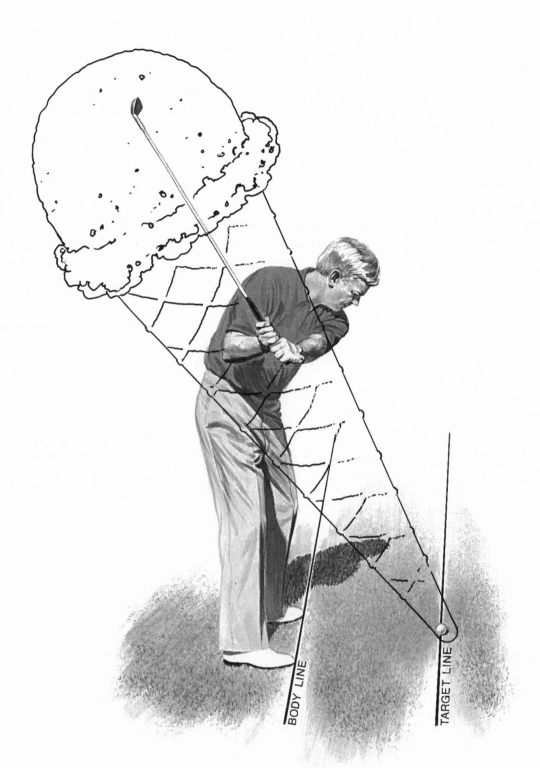

BODY LINE

TARGET LINE

NO PLANE, NO GAIN
THE IMPORTANCE OF SWINGING THE CLUB ON PLANE

It's no coincidence that this chapter on swing plane directly follows our discussion of body motion. To swing the club "on plane" throughout the golf swing—powerfully—you must pivot your body properly. *The start of the downswing is the make-or-break point for swing plane. Players who move their bodies in the proper sequence when starting downward movement are much more likely to deliver the clubshaft on plane, swing after swing.*

The actual plane angle of the swing differs from golfer to golfer, because of variances in stature. Plane differs from shot to shot too, because of differences in the lie of the ball and/or the lie angle of the club. All the same, there is still an ironclad cause-and-effect relationship between pivoting properly and swinging powerfully on the established plane. Sequencing the body movements properly allows the club to fall into place much easier without hand or arm manipulation.

As vital as it is, the concept of plane intimidates a lot of golfers. In part, this is because most discussions of swing plane are vague and incomplete. What is it that the golfer should try to swing on plane? The hands? The arms? One answer would be the clubhead. A more accurate answer would be the *clubshaft*. In the process of keeping the clubshaft on plane, the hands, arms, and shoulders might also move on plane. And there will certainly be points in the swing at which the plane established by your left arm or your hands will be the same as the plane the clubshaft moves along. For sure, the hands, arms, and shoulders all play a major role in keeping the clubshaft and clubhead on plane.

In many a misleading illustration, the plane of the golf swing is shown as a shadowed area, resembling a sheet of glass, that rests on the golfer's shoulders. Since Ben Hogan's book *Five Lessons* was published in 1957, that imaginary pane of glass has been shown extending upward from the ball through the golfer's hands and passing over the shoulders, with a small hole for his or her head. This classic diagram does *not* tell the whole story of swing plane. It correctly shows the ideal swing plane for the left arm and the clubshaft during the middle period of the swing and up to the top of the backswing. But before you start thinking about whether your swing coincides with this venerable diagram, take a look at another image. What you're looking at in the figure at right is the first plane, or "address plane," of the swing.

The address plane of the swing is the line we draw along the shaft as it sits at address and might also be termed the "shaft plane." This plane relates to how the clubhead travels up and down from the ball, to a point that's waist high. In this limited arc, you're either on plane, over the plane, or under the plane. It's one of those three things. One of many statements in Hogan's book about the plane that was completely correct, incidentally, is that the baseline of the swing plane is the line extending from the target back through the ball and continuing farther backward. *That line, the target line, is the most important line in golf.*

The dotted line represents the Address Shaft Plane.

Between the address plane and what we'll call the "Hogan plane," something happens. Your hands, if you were to view them from behind, usually veer upward in a curving path, leaving that lower plane and rising to the Hogan plane. There are exceptions to this rule, but it is still a solid observation.

All in all, there is no question that swing plane is overrated in relation to the backswing. There are many different ways to take the club back that are acceptable. What's important during the take-away are the body movements that get you started and the absence of tension in the arms, wrists, and hands. Of course, if the club goes right up the address shaft plane line, it is tracking back on a model swing arc. However, it is much more important that we do not destroy the naturalness of movement. If the club tends to rise a bit above the address plane line or drop below it slightly, we should have no problem getting to an adequate backswing position. Staying within this liberal *Corridor of Success* allows you to reach a position of leverage from which you can swing the club powerfully and, most important, on plane in the downswing.

RECONCILING THE TWO PLANES OF THE BACKSWING WITH THE PLANE OF THE DOWNSWING

Going back to our address shaft plane diagram, we can plot another plane line, one that equates to the plane in Hogan's book. Drawn here on the same page together (see page 26), the two lines form a triangle or ice cream cone, which is an image I picked up from Denis Pugh, one of Europe's top golf instructors. In evaluating the plane of a student's swing, I check to see if he or she stays within this *safety zone*.

The right elbow is the one part of your body that most tends to sneak out of the safety zone. I don't ever like to see the right elbow underneath the address plane line. That often indicates that the arms have been pulled inside too much or that the right elbow has connected to the body in the backswing and remained connected. This also indicates that the left arm has gone completely across the golfer's chest. All are bad mistakes. These actions violate one of my general principles: *keep the arms in front of your body center throughout the swing.*

You've seen clearly that two separate planes occur in the backswing, and that most golfers elevate their hands (left arm) up and out of the address plane and close to the shoulder plane. You may wonder if a similar lowering and retracking of the hands take place on the downswing. The answer is *no.* For a host of reasons, the plane of the hands in the downswing does not retrack the "ripple," or dish-shaped upward curve, in the middle of the backswing. Gravity, increased swing speed, and

the quick lowering motion at the *beginning* of the downswing make the arm-and-hand plane steeper and usually slightly outside the backswing arc. It is also more consistent than the backswing plane and is not dish shaped. Interestingly, the shaft plane works in just the *opposite* way. The plane of the clubshaft actually flattens on the downswing. This mirrors the baseball batter as he or she strides forward into the hitting zone. The baseball bat falls and "flattens" visibly. The top golfers will follow this natural fall-down action as well.

OPPOSITE

Like the baseball batter's plane of swing, the golfer's plane of swing flattens as he moves into the hitting area.

RIGHT

The end of the club that is closer to the ground should point at the target line.

Here are two simple ways for you to think about swing plane and how you can monitor it:

An on-plane swing (left); an off-plane swing (right).

● Remember that the end of the club that is closer to the ground always points to the target line. There are four important points in a model swing when the shaft is parallel to the target line: halfway back, at the top, halfway down, and halfway up to the follow-through finish. When the club is at address or impact, or near to either, the end of the shaft should point directly at the target line. When the grip end of the club is closer to the ground, the grip end of the shaft should, indeed, be pointed at that target line.

● Check how sensitive the on-plane swing is to small muscle movements by sticking a tee in the vent hole of the grip and slowly swinging the club backward. Stop when your left arm is parallel to the ground and the club is set. Ideally, the tee will be aimed directly at the target line. Now rotate your wrists just a small amount and notice how far the tee moves off its original angle. The great amount of variance you see confirms that swinging on plane is a high-precision movement.

DEATH MOVE: THE TIPPED-OVER SHAFT

I have said that proper swing plane is the result of many sound, proper positions and movements. If you want to play golf in a clear-minded athletic manner, which is how the game should be played, you probably do not want to think intently about swing plane. *In general, checking your plane is a diagnostic measure that a coach or instructor does for you.* However, you can easily work on plane improvement by watching in a mirror at home or by doing drills prescribed by your teacher to help you overcome off-plane swinging automatically.

A flat backswing axis (left); shoulders turning on the correct axis (right).

If you are more comfortable leaving the whole issue of plane to your pro or teacher, you may want to skip the in-depth descriptions that follow. But don't skip on to another chapter without understanding the one *Death Move* associated with swing plane. I call it the "tipped-over" shaft. When you tip the shaft over in your forward swing, you trap yourself in a position from which there is little or no escape. The shot you hit will almost certainly be a high, weak slice and if not that, a low pull.

Tipping that shaft over on the forward swing (so that the tee in the vent hole points to a line that runs through your toes instead of the line the ball rests on), is truly a *Death Move*. Very often, the swing that produces this tip over is too flat going back and then too upright (or steep) coming down into the forward swing. The shaft is working in the opposite fashion from a top ball striker.

SUMMARY: BUILDING BLOCKS OF ON-PLANE SWINGING

In the general order of occurrence during the swing, here are the fundamental points of swing plane.

1. There are few, if any golfers in the world who move the clubshaft/clubhead along exactly the same plane during the backswing and the downswing. The downswing is always narrower than the backswing.
2. Just because your swing is on plane in the backswing in no way ensures that you will be on plane in the downswing.
3. If you look at the shaft alone, you'll see that most top golfers move up on a plane that is steeper than the plane they come down along. In any case, the downswing plane is more critical than the backswing plane. As noted, the shaft plane flattens on the downswing.
4. In cases in which a player's backswing and forward swing have been coached to move closer to the same plane, the player's accuracy and ball striking generally show a noticeable improvement.

5 There is not a single ideal swing plane that suits all golfers. The amount of individualism in peoples' swings may prevent that from ever being so. But all players (with the help of a knowledgeable instructor) can understand plane and make critical improvements that bring them closer to the model swing—again, especially on the downward swing of the club. I hope that a careful study of this chapter will allow you better to understand and identify swing plane.

6 The better the ball striker, the better the plane. There truly is a correlation between playing ability and how well a golfer swings on plane. Most low handicappers move the club in a way that is much closer to being on plane than high handicappers.

7 Making swing changes to get the club to move on plane takes hard work and proper practice. Any prompt correction of a poor plane will take accurate video work, practicing in front of mirrors, and a tremendous number of practice swings. However, if you can consistently get your club on plane in the downswing, you will greatly improve your chances of accurate ball striking.

8 Establishing accurate alignments during the setup is critical to starting the club on plane. Aligning your body in different ways will definitely change your plane tendencies. For example, aim left = shallow plane, aim right = steeper plane. This is a general rule.

9 The right elbow and proper shoulder rotation have much to do with how the club moves on plane. It is most important that the golfer employ the downswing in the correct shift-rotate-hit sequence. As the lower body begins the forward swing, the right elbow and right shoulder will lower and the clubshaft will flatten. This adherence to the laws of human motion corrects many a downswing plane flaw.

10 As I stated, the backswing tends to have two basic planes. Stand behind a skilled golfer. You will see, perhaps to your surprise, that the hands rise up along a curving arc; they do not swing back along Hogan's sheet of glass. If you attempt to swing your hands along that sheet of glass, you will most likely flirt with the *Death Move*.

⑪ The slight lateral motion that most great players have in their back swing keeps them on plane without stealing the athletic quality of their swing. Focusing on a steady head (i.e., no movement) often leads to overuse of the arms and lifting the arms over the plane.

⑫ It is possible to have a perfect swing arc, to be right on plane, yet have either a weak and/or inconsistent swing. This can happen with bad body motion or inconsistent control of the clubface.

⑬ After impact, the club must swing back to the left. It must not be forced down the target line.

UNDERSTANDING PLANE ANGLE

I have discussed a model swing plane. It is constant and causes a swing that is, in theory, perfect. Now I would like to bring up a subject that is not constant—and is thus a source of much confusion—*plane angle*. Plane angle is the angle between the ground and that part of your body or your equipment that is (or ought to be) moving along a desired flat path. And when I say *desired*, I am taking into account the "situation" of the shot. For example, the plane angle of a nine iron is steeper than the plane angle of a driver and a five iron. Similarly, the plane angle is steeper with the same club when the ball is below the feet than when the ball is above the feet.

So although the plane is relatively constant for each club and the swing is relatively constant, the plane angle changes from shot to shot, based on the slope of your lie and the club you've selected.

The plane angle differs from club to club.

Learning to swing on plane is a requirement for a precision swing that will repeat itself under the pressure of competition.

If you follow the fundamentals of human motion and make a true swinging action, you will put your club on plane shot after shot. Clearing up the confusion over plane is an important first step, but practice and frequent lesson checkups (especially with video) are the best ways to develop for yourself a solidly on-plane swing.

CLUB CONTROL
THERE ARE TWO DISTINCT WAYS TO MOVE THE GOLF CLUB

When practice-range spectators gather behind tour players and watch them hit one long, accurate drive after another, someone in the gallery will usually utter the question: "How do they *do* that?" If they happen to be watching Ian Woosnam, Jeff Sluman, Bill Britton, or some other player of lesser physical stature, they will probably ask: "Where does all that *power* come from?"

You can watch all day, but you will likely never really know where the golf swing's power, control, and leverage come from until you *feel it yourself.* A golf instructor's best moments occur when the students finally feel themselves swinging the club in a way that makes *full* use of their physical ability. Golf is as dissimilar as it can be from such clear-cut athletic acts as doing a bench press in weight lifting. Unlike such starkly obvious functions, golf demands a complex series of movements to maximize the athlete's latent energy and apply it to the object to be moved.

In trying to take the invisible interconnections of the golf swing and make them visible to people, I sometimes use the following phrases: *the body hits the ball, the arms guide the club, and the hands fine-tune.*

Technically speaking, of course, the body cannot hit the ball, because the clubhead hits the ball, and the body is connected to the clubhead only via the arms and hands. While this fact may be obvious to a first-time spectator, the real workings of the golf swing are not. To me, there are two distinct ways in which the body becomes involved in the swing motion:

- The hands and arms dominate.
- The hands, arms, and club respond to the body.

DIFFERENT CONCEPTS

BACKSWING MOTIONS AND FEEL

OPTION 1

The hands and arms dominate. They start the club back, and the large muscles of your upper body and your legs *follow* the club, or *give*, with the swing. The body is thus responding—immediately—to the swinging action created by the arms. This type of action is best illustrated in the swings of a first-rate female golfer or junior golfer. Their swings tend to be characterized by complete freedom of motion. Fred Couples and Meg Mallon are examples of professional golfers who exhibit this free-arm swing.

OPTION 2

The hands, arms, and club respond to the body. Here the hands and arms move as a result of motion originating in the torso, trunk, and legs. To be specific, the large muscles through the

LEFT
Fred Couples: The ultimate free-arm swinger.

RIGHT
Gary Player: A classic body swinger.

shoulders, often helped by a push off the inside of the left leg or left instep, initiate the backswing and put the arms and hands in motion.

As you can see, Option 2 is quite different from Option 1. In this second option, the body *center* dominates the take-away. It serves as an inner engine to start the swing. Prime examples of contemporary players who employ this method are Jack Nicklaus, Nick Faldo, Gary Player, and Nick Price. In the past, Ben Hogan, Ken Venturi, and Byron Nelson controlled their backswing with this one-piece take-away motion.

THE SEQUENCE OF LEARNING

In the hands-and-arms technique, the golfer feels the hands dominating the movements. This is by far the best way to learn the golf swing as a beginner. If he or she feels the body's involvement at all, it is perceived to play a supporting role. I believe it is correct for beginners and many intermediate golfers to "feel" the backswing in this manner. The reason is simple: we train ourselves in steps and stages. We crawl, walk, run, and then finally we race. *Golfers should feel and learn through their hands first.* You start by training your hands to move to specific locations or by copying the swing action of an accomplished player. *You learn to control and square the clubface with your hands.* Next, you train the arms to make a tension-free motion. Finally, you connect the hands, arms, and body motions into your swing center to become the best and most powerful player you can be.

THE ARMS GUIDE THE CLUB,
THE HANDS FINE-TUNE

The second option for take-away and backswing, you'll remember, calls on the body, or the swing center, to initiate or begin the backswing motion and create a free-swinging action of the arms. There is no thought or intent to guide the club into a position with the hands. The arms and hands do virtually nothing. They go along for the ride. The feeling is that they are "slung away." In Jimmy Ballard's oft-quoted words, "The dog is wagging the tail." I like to see the upper body and sometimes the left knee create a slight *lateral move* that puts the arms and club into motion. With grip pressure relatively light, the club is almost flung into the backswing, in a totally connected responsive action.

This is the desired feeling for a seasoned player, even if he or she remains faintly conscious of the hands and arms keeping the club on its path. As you can see, we are training the hands for golf by consciously and gradually getting them to do less and less. Beginners learn to control the swing with their hands and arms, whereas experts come to have no conscious feeling of hand manipulation whatsoever. Advanced players have trained their hands and arms. The workings of the hands are second nature and happen automatically. Ideally, the top player will feel the hands remaining in the address position throughout the entire swing motion. He or she will also feel the wrists hinge vertically. But this is a high-level skill that takes years to attain.

A POWERFUL, ACCURATE BACKSWING: THE VIEW FROM FORTY-FIVE DEGREES

Those spectators on the practice range would discern the power connections in the swing a little better if they stood facing the tour player but at an angle of about forty-five degrees off point blank, toward the target. I particularly like this angle because there is a strong image of the upper body's full coil. It is especially noticeable in the windup of the left shoulder. The left shoulder muscles (the "lats" and "pecs") coil and appear to make a massive move back behind the golf ball. At the same time, the left leg appears to move—its movements look synchronized with the move of the left shoulder, but whether the leg initiates or responds is difficult to ascertain.

It is very clear that the actions of these two muscle groups are tightly coordinated. The forty-five degree angle view provides one of the best possible glimpses of the body's creation of energy to move the club on the backswing. The entire left side is seen winding the club up and behind the golfer. The clubshaft and clubhead, again, appear to be *slung* into the backswing. The relationship of the arms to the body has not changed from address; and we witness the *one-piece take-away*.

With the body creating the swinging action, this natural athletic move happens over and over; *it repeats easily*. Coming from the center and moving outward, the force can build and flow consistently. Therefore, the player builds a swing that can be trusted not to break down under the pressure of competition. Furthermore, with the body (rather than the hands and arms) initiating the motions, the golfer doesn't have to be concerned with specific positions; that's because the triangle formed at address is maintained through the first stage of the swing. Of course, mastering that feel for the swing is not easy. If it were, everyone would be a great ball striker. Mastering feel takes time and practice. Only after a period of dedicated and proper practice does it seem to become clear and simple. In the end, it is the most efficient pressure-proof swing, and it is truly easier to repeat.

THE POSITION AT THE TOP

Moving on to the body's role in the downswing, I'm reminded of something Jackie Burke said more than twenty years ago: "Check the top five money winners each year. Look at their positions at the top of the backswing. Every year you will see five different positions."

Since that time, I have checked every year, and so far the statement has held true. The upshot is this: if there were a magic position at the top of the backswing that would guarantee all of us great golf shots, you can bet I would be swinging to that position and teaching all of my students to swing to that position, and so would every other instructor! But there is no one perfect at-the-top position. Getting to a certain position at the top will work for some players, but it absolutely does not spell success for all golfers. An exact location or position of the hands at the completion of the backswing is *not* a fundamental.

DOWNSWING MOTIONS AND FEEL

To reverse the direction of the club (from backswing to downswing), let's again compare the hands-and-arms–dominated motion with the body-dominated motion. But before going any further, we will continue the previous point by stating this absolute: *it is the position of the clubface as the club starts down that is critical. At this point in the swing, the clubface cannot be shut or be extremely open—in what I call a* Death Position—*where no recovery is possible.*

In an efficient downswing that is dominated by the hands and arms, the arms initiate a free swing down toward the ball, with the body responding. The feeling is of complete freedom and abandonment. The accomplished junior golfer is the classic example of this motion. Juniors usually have swings in which the loose, swooping action of the club pulls the body around to a full, upright follow-through. There is nothing wrong with this type of action, and I totally recommend it for a beginner. The hips react to the hands. Many baseball coaches teach a hitting motion in the same way, especially if the batter is opening the body prematurely. This is a swing that will promote "draw" shots.

In a swing dominated by the body, opposite actions occur, yet the results can be the same. I just think this is by far the best method under pressure. The force that reverses the swing's direction from back to forward comes first from the lower body and is relayed immediately through the upper body. The last thing to change direction is the clubhead. To do this, there may be a feeling of the knees shifting laterally. The player may pump or kick off the right foot. There may be a feeling of the hips unwinding. Whatever the feel, the hands and arms are passive. They are put into motion by the weight transfer and rotation of the body. As a result, the arms, hands, and club lag behind, and begin a virtual free fall downward.

A correct sequence of body motion allows the right elbow automatically to tuck into the right side. The club is definitely on an inside *attack track*, or slot, at the point we consider halfway from the top to impact. The weight shift forward and the right elbow tuck are tremendously valuable swing thoughts. These two movements happen in unison. Linking them together into a single motion connects the arms and body and delivers them into perfect hitting position. Harvey Penick is one teacher who had success with students, because he had

Sense that the club "falls" freely downward during the change of direction. At this point the club should be square or even slightly open.

them learn and groove these synchronized vital movements of the downswing, often in *slow motion.*

The only action required by the golfer from this point is to continue forward through the ball to a balanced finish, with 100 percent of the weight moving to the front foot. Centrifugal force, gravity, and an uninhibited free-swinging action square the clubhead. There is no conscious manipulation of the club with the hands, as the turn of the body squares the clubface to the ball. This is the "no-hands" feeling top players describe. If there is a conscious thought by the top players, it is to have solid hands and *an absence of hand manipulation through the ball.*

The clubhead speed generated by this process is always a pleasant surprise to the average golfer, who tends to see club-head speed as a product of consciously increased hand-and-arm–swinging speed. It is the body that ignites the arms. Actually, maximum clubhead velocity is a by-product of *passive hands and arms.*

Part of trusting these physical facts is resisting the urge to throw or thrust the clubhead out at the ball through impact. As you'll soon realize through hard practice, the clubhead can get out to the ball simply by rotating your body center. There is no need to throw the hands out at the ball, although this is an incredibly strong impulse.

THE ARMS GUIDE THE CLUB

Because the arms are attached to the body at the shoulder joints and the hands/wrists are the connection between the arms and the club, it is the arms that should direct the path of the club

The shift action creates an inside-to-inside elongated "flat" spot in the swing.

throughout the swing. If the arms do nothing but stay in front of the player's chest throughout the swing, and if he or she has correct ball position and correct body motions, the club must swing on an inside-to-inside arc. *The shift action from the right foot to the left foot allows a long flatter spot and a longer on-line motion—still, of course, inside-to-inside.*

SHOULDER ROTATION

To clarify further the role of the arms in directing the path of the club, it should be kept in mind that in a model swing the shoulders rotate at a ninety degree angle to the spine angle. This is a very natural path for the shoulders to follow and introduces no artificial angles or club manipulation during the backswing or forward swing. The shoulders turn on an axis and there must be a smooth and constant rotation through to the finish. This puts the clubshaft on a completely natural—and therefore, repeatable—plane. The arms, then, have no choice but to respond to the motions of the body.

It is important to note that the right shoulder lowers because the lower body *initiates the forward movement.* The better player needs to avoid conscious efforts to lower the right shoulder too much by sliding the lower body laterally, because this action creates a swing plane that's too deep from the inside. See page 120: Swing Left to Swing Right.

Clubface control, by the hands, becomes far easier under the passive-arms, passive-hands approach. However, it does demand proper use of the body. By keeping the hands unified with constant grip pressure, you relegate the left hand and left wrist to a single responsibility: *not to break down!* Inward bending of the left wrist before impact is probably the biggest power leak in the swing. When the hands are in sync, there is no requirement for independent wrist action or for any conscious use of the hands to manipulate the clubface to produce your normal repeating ball flight.

It's my observation that the greatest players in history have particularly emphasized "no hands" when speaking about their swings. Does this mean they had no hand action? Of course it doesn't. To be great players, they had to have their hands

In looking at these four illustrations, note the changing role of shoulder-rotation during the swing.

working and releasing perfectly. *What it does mean is that they were not aware of their hands.* They did not have to think about hand action. Their hands and wrists were trained and had no responsibility in the swing other than to hold on and go along for the ride. The feeling is that the hands maintain the address position throughout the swing. The hands responded automatically to the exquisite body motion of the great golfers.

THE HANDS FINE-TUNE

When it comes to specialty shots and purposely curved shots, of course, conscious hand action and variations in grip pressure do come into play. To hit a low slice or high hook, the player will use the hands differently from the way he or she hits a standard shot. Partially through setup, partially through visualization, and partially through a conscious swing thought that includes wrist/hand action, the player will adjust to the special situation. The hands come into these special predicaments and *fine-tune* the swing action to produce various curving shots.

WHERE TIMING COMES IN

Under pressure of competition, a swing whose tempo and timing is controlled by the big muscles will be more reliable. Logic alone will tell you that trying to time the hands when the heat is on is a tough task. Many great players, particularly Ben Hogan and Jack Nicklaus, have talked or written about the no-hands feeling. When it's time to fine-tune the swing to produce hooks, slices, high shots, and low shots, the hands are there to hold the club differently, to vary the grip pressure, to hold on through impact (block release), or otherwise to play a part. From Step Five in my Eight-Step Swing system, it's as if the hands did nothing; a strong body turn is what enables the golfer to hammer the ball.

IT'S ROUTINE
A GOOD SET UP PROCEDURE WILL
HELP YOU PRODUCE A GOOD SHOT

To the tour professional, a shot routine that begins the second he or she identifies the ball and starts analyzing the lie and ends with the swing is an essential part of the game that is taken very seriously. The professional knows that all the detailed preparatory work relative to planning a shot has a direct influence on the result. If the golfer goes through a very thorough process of surveying the on-course situation and also visualizes a good shot vividly before swinging, there's an excellent chance that he or she will hit that good shot and be putting for a birdie.

In the case of the typical amateur, many shots are missed before they are played. Why? Due to passiveness or neglect (or ignorance), the average golfer fails to do carefully such vital things as assess the lie, survey the target area, identify the target line, and practice or visualize the swing he or she intends to make when it comes time to hit the ball. The golfer eventually "sets up for failure." Don't you make the same mistakes. Instead, adhere to a set shot procedure.

The following routine is not complex, but it is thorough. It is used for every shot and only encompasses that brief period (fifteen to forty-five seconds) during which you are preparing for and executing the shot. For the remainder of the time between shots, relax and have fun with the people in your group. If you make the effort to practice the preshot routine sequence until it is ingrained, you *will* see improvement in your play.

THE ROUTINE

PROCEDURE ONE: PREPARE

A golf course is a diverse environment full of subtleties and sur-
prises. Whether you generally strike the ball seventy times or
one hundred times per round, you should devote serious attention to circumstances surrounding your ball—including the lie,
distances, and conditions—and the results you want to achieve.
Good players notice everything. They don't miss a thing, taking
in all pertinent information. The best way to analyze all the variables is to break them down individually, as follows.

LEFT
*An uneven lie will change the
plane of your golf swing.*

RIGHT
*Assess all information; here
checking wind direction.*

Ⓐ *Identify Your Ball.* Make sure the ball you're getting ready
to hit is yours. If you hit the wrong ball in a match-play
event, you automatically lose the hole. If you hit the
wrong ball (except in a hazard) during a stroke-play
event, you will be penalized two strokes. Smart players

personalize their ball before playing, by putting a marking (e.g., an *X* or three dots) on it with a pencil or pen. The reason: there are many balls with the same brand name and number.

Ⓑ *Analyze the Lie.* Look at the slope of the land, examine the type of grass you're hitting from and the direction it grows, determine if the grass is wet or dry, determine whether there is hardpan underneath the ball, and so on. An experienced player makes judgments like these in an instant.

Ⓒ *Check Your Surroundings.* Determine whether the stance you'll take will affect any of your positions at address.

LEFT

When hitting to a blind green, it's particularly important to pick a target along the line to the hole, such as a tree in the distance.

RIGHT

In preparing to swing, take an extra second to check for "exit" areas near the green.

Ⓓ *Check Wind Direction and Wind Speed.* Although you should determine the direction of the prevailing wind before teeing off, be careful to not be fooled by flags on greens that are still. They may be blocked by tall trees. Look at the tops of the trees to see if there is wind that will affect your shot.

E *Identify Your Target Line.* Identifying the target line will allow you to set properly all of your body alignments. Many golfers choose an intermediate target from one foot to several yards ahead of their ball, on the target line.

F *Survey the Target Area.* Is the target area flat, sloping, hard, or soft? Check for your "exit area"—the spot where you'd prefer a mishit shot to land. Generally, though not always, one side of the green is more clear of trouble or severe slopes. There are many course situations that call for a more safe play, even for the fine player. For instance, Jack Nicklaus plays to the center of many greens and always clearly analyzes the surrounding safe spots.

G *Determine Distance.* The tournament player must be exact and not estimate, must always be aware of the distance to the front edge of the green, and must "carry" yardage over bunkers or water. Such a golfer also must be aware of the depth of the green (front to back) and know the distances to different levels or severe slopes in the green.

A yardage pad or booklet will help you hit shots the correct distance.

PROCEDURE TWO: VISUALIZE

In your mind, picture the ball leaving and taking a specific trajectory to the target area. If you have any difficulty seeing the shot, simply ask yourself, "What am I trying to do?" Clarity is essential at this point. You must make a pure commitment to your target and have a precise idea of what type of shot you are planning to play.

Dr. Dick Coop, with whom I have conducted some golf schools, has convinced many of the top players in the world that their preshot routine can start with a conscious cue. This cue is your signal to focus on the situation at hand. For the next twenty to thirty seconds, your concentration and visualization button is turned on. Some, but certainly not all, golfers benefit greatly by using a conscious cue. Your cue should be some physical act. Golfers who have difficulty with the preshot routine may be helped greatly by using a conscious act or even an audible sound. Here are some examples:

(A) Release then reclose the Velcro closure on your glove—this provides an act and a sound together.

(B) Tug outward on your shirt and release; do this twice rapidly to produce an act and a sound together.

(C) Remove and replace your cap—no sound with this cue.

Be sure to change your cue periodically. You want your cue to be a conscious act, not an unconscious habit. It is done to get you into the "ignition" mode. It causes you to say, "I am going to focus on this shot completely for the next twenty seconds."

A conscious cue, such as releasing the Velcro on your glove (left), tugging on your shirt (center), or removing your cap (right), can be used to trigger intense concentration prior to the preshot routine.

PROCEDURE THREE: RELAX

Stand to the rear of the ball and take a cleansing breath. Exhale twice as slowly as you inhaled. You may want to shake your arms and fingers a bit if you feel extra tension. Use these simple ideas or any other relaxation techniques to get yourself prepared to play. But remember, a relaxed body and a quiet mind are the keys to *peak* performance. Also, it is very possible to be nervous, yet physically relaxed.

Promote relaxation by standing behind the ball and breathing extra slowly. This begins your approach to the set up position.

PROCEDURE FOUR: PROCESS YOUR DATA

Based on the data, make the club selection that will give you the results you desire.

It's important *not* to choose a club until you have produced a very vivid mental picture of the shot you intend to hit. While on this subject, let me make sure to say this clearly: *don't overdo this procedure.* You can make all of this preshot routine too detailed and overimportant.

When I played on the golf team at the University of Houston, our coach, Dave Williams (seventeen NCAA championships), would become livid if one of his players made too much of the preswing analysis. When a player used the excuse of poor yardage and/or incomplete preparation, Coach would scream, "If you can play this game, you can pick any club. Just take out any club and hit the ball at the flagstick! But don't make excuses and don't be indecisive. And don't ever *look* indecisive." At first glance, this advice may seem farfetched, but believe me, there is truth in those words. *If you can play, you'll be decisive. Your preshot routine will be clear. Too much thinking is just as bad as no thinking—in fact, sometimes much worse.*

PROCEDURE FIVE: "SEE" THE SWING

Form a mental image of the swing. For some folks, this will be detailed and clear. For others it will be automatic and sensed via "feel."

PROCEDURE SIX: PHYSICALLY PRACTICE THE SWING MOTION

Move to the side of the ball. Generally set your alignments and take an effortless practice swing.

LEFT
Good club selection means knowing your game.

RIGHT
To promote good shots, first visualize your best swing.

Most top players just use a practice motion to release tension and prep themselves. You may want to make the practice swing that is an exact duplicate of the swing you intend to put on the ball. This is a good idea, because it gives your brain a chance to confirm or reject the strategy of your planned swing. I especially like this procedure for tough shots around the green.

PROCEDURE SEVEN: GET SET, LOOK TWICE, GO

I recommend you approach the ball from behind, with your eyes looking at the target. Then either (1) place both hands on the club, feel and sense your grip pressure, and place the clubhead behind the ball or (2) hold the club in the right hand, step into the "golfer's box" with your right foot to begin the alignment procedure, and set the club behind the ball. This second procedure, used by many great players, is the most natural and most logical too, because it ensures that you are "open," which gives you a better visual perspective of the target.

Make your practice swing count.

After setting the club down, set your feet and body into their correct alignment positions, according to the directions given at the end of this chapter.

Next, look intently at the target, then glance quickly at the ball, while still jockeying your feet into position. Repeat the look-glance procedure, then go! I say, "One look to the target, two looks to the target, set, and go"—a proven procedure I stole from the great Johnny Revolta. Watch and see how many top pro golfers instinctively use this simple prehit routine.

Good players stare at the target and stay in motion. High handicappers do just the opposite. They stare at the ball and have no motion in the lower body. The ball is the most important thing in the world to the poor player.

Tailoring the Tip. Good players stare at the target and glance at the ball; poor players glance at the target and stare at the ball.

PROCEDURE EIGHT: EVALUATE YOUR SHOT

Rate the shot; good or bad, make the swing part of your database. Learn from your successes; learn from your mistakes.

It is a bad mistake to miss this evaluation process after each swing. Ideally, you should do this even while practicing on the range. Complete your swing, reflex the club to your hold position, and then watch your golf ball fly. Allow your brain to process the information and feed the computer new valuable information. This will prevent you from repeating the same mistake, hole after hole.

LEFT

Learn to step into the shot, right foot first, as most great right-handed players do.

RIGHT

After each shot, hold the finish and evaluate it.

REMINDERS AND HINTS

1 If any distraction causes you to lose your mental image at any point during the routine, you should discipline yourself and return to the first step and start the entire routine over again. I'm not talking about minor distractions. If little things are bothering you, then your concentration is poor. You'll never be a top-notch player if you can't "zone out" playing partners or other normal noise and movements.

2 Train yourself to avoid programming negative information—bunkers, water hazards, out-of-bounds, and so

on—into your preshot thinking. Don't overanalyze. Stay positively focused on your target. This is the time to use Harvey Penick's famous thought: "Take dead aim."

3 At first, you may need to be precise and methodical. Do your best not to omit any information or any part of your procedure. The shot performance you achieve is the result of what your brain has told your body to do. The better the information, the better the result. With time, this information-gathering sequence will become fast and efficient.

4 Stay confident and focused no matter how difficult the course situation. Tough situations set up great recovery opportunities. Remember, some of golf's finest players, such as Arnold Palmer, Tom Watson, and Seve Ballesteros, were at their best from trouble situations.

5 *Let* it happen. Don't try to make it happen. No advice I can give is more important.

6 Don't get discouraged by a bad shot. Concentrate on what to do "right" on the next swing and go forward.

7 Good habits can be learned. The more you practice concentration and visualization, the better your preshot routine becomes. You may have to start with a six-inch putt and work your way up to the driver, but practice will get you there.

8 Dr. Fran Pirozzolo, neurologist and sports psychologist, points out that, out of 250 to 300 minutes elapsed time in a competitive round, the golfer is concentrating on a shot for only 48 minutes. That's a ratio we can all handle.

9 Finally, if a negative thought or image pops inside your head, use this great technique I learned from both Ken Venturi and Dr. Pirozzolo. You may say to yourself, for example, "Don't hit the ball into the lake on the right." Because your brain sees pictures, *don't* is not powerful, whereas *lake* is. Instead, say to yourself, "I see the lake, so I'll hit it hard at the distant fir tree behind the mound." You have thus replaced a negative with a *positive* last thought. And you'd better believe that last thought before you swing is the most critical.

THE SET: A KEY GOLF FUNDAMENTAL

I often refer to the address routine as the *set* instead of the setup. I compare the golfer's need to go through a preshot routine, stand up to the ball, and then swing with a sprinter's need to take the mark, get set, and go. I don't look at the set as a separate item to be taught alone. I prefer to incorporate it into my instruction on the preshot routine. When players have gone through their preshot routine properly, they know the shot they want to hit and the ball flight they desire. But these decisions can only be carried out if the players get set to the ball in a manner that suits the shot.

Hitting extra tee shots will improve your driving skills.

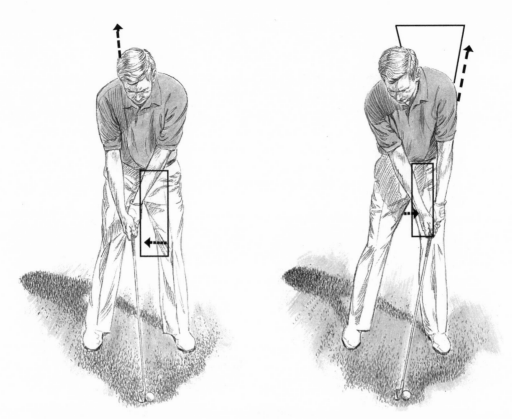

Tailoring the Tip. At address, you are bent over at the waist slightly with your knees flexed and "live tension" in your legs. Both feet are flat on the ground, and your weight is equally distributed on the entire foot, from the ball back to the heel. Usually, too, your hips are square to the target line, with the hip "girdles" pushed outward and the hip "pockets" four to eight inches outside your heels. The clubhead is normally in line with the hands, or within the allowable *Corridor of Success*.

Ideally, the butt of the club points between your navel and the crease of your slacks. Deviating from this configuration is not recommended. As long as you keep the hands and the club's handle between your body center and the crease of your slacks, you are within the acceptable parameters.

In setting up, be careful not to let your hands drift too far behind (left), or too far ahead (right). The "corridor of success" is identified on this and subsequent photos.

SET YOUR BODY "PARALLEL LEFT"

Regardless of the skill level of the amateur golfer I am working with, I initially want him or her to set up *parallel* to the ball-to-target line. I use the popular image of the railroad tracks to get this point across. The ball/target line is the outside rail, and the inside rail is the line the player uses to set the body alignments. This mental picture is widely used because it is virtually foolproof. Plus it presents a vividly clear mental picture that all students can easily relate to.

Along that inside rail, students should set their eyes, shoulders, hips, knees, forearms, and feet. Minor adjustments to this initial parallel model can be made with time. To simplify it, remember that the arms, which connect to the club, are attached to the shoulders. Therefore, the alignment of the shoulders is most critical of all. Rarely, if ever, will I set the shoulders closed. It is clear that the great ball hitters set the upper body parallel to the target line, or significantly more open, never closed. Interestingly, some of the great tour players whom I've studied closely set up closed with the lower body, open with the upper body—especially with the longer clubs.

Ball position varies from shot to shot, depending upon endless variables.

ONE BALL POSITION FOR EVERY SHOT? NO WAY!

This is the obvious rebuttal to advocates of the "one-ball-position-for-every-shot" theory. To me, it is absolutely ludicrous to think you can play all shots from one position in your stance. Not only is most every shot you hit on the golf course from a different lie, often you have particular wind conditions and pin locations that require you to hit a low shot, high shot, draw, hook, fade, or slice. Instead of changing your entire swing and weight distribution for every shot, simply change the ball position. To hit different shots requires that you change something. To me, it is obvious that the easiest change is—*ball position*.

Let's have a reality check. To hit a short iron on a pure "tour-pro" trajectory—that is, relatively low with maximum backspin—will require a different striking action from a drive hit off a tee from a flat stance. Of course, you could play that short iron off your left heel or instep, as one-ball-position advocates suggest. But then you'd also have to put 70 percent of your weight on your forward foot at address, set up with your hands well ahead of the ball, increase your grip pressure, make a huge lateral move into the ball on the downswing, concentrate extra hard on keeping your hands way ahead of the clubhead in the hitting area, and drive the clubhead low through and well past the ball.

Wouldn't you rather just move the ball back in your stance and make a shorter, firmer version of your normal swing to hit this shot? Of course you would.

On paper, to a theorist, playing the ball from one position for all shots may seem like a good idea. To an accomplished player, it's a joke. Even if tour players tell you that they play the ball from the same point in their stance on every shot, don't believe them. Typical pros have played golf almost their entire lives and, therefore, must be making automatic adjustments to different playing circumstances. If these adjustments are second nature to you as well, you can go right on thinking you play every shot from the same spot. Just don't start doing it.

Ball position moves from the center of your stance for wedges, up to the left heel for the driver. The width of stance makes exact positioning off any part of the body impractical.

ALIGNMENT TELLS THE TALE

Often, the harder you work on your swing, the tougher it is for you to believe that most golf shots are missed even before the swing begins. Be that as it may, a poor shot often is the result of poor alignment in the setup. Ken Venturi always drilled home the point that golfers don't lose their swing so much as they *lose their position at address.* "They don't get out of swing, they get out of position." Ken always hammered that point home. The more I've taught, the more I agree.

Alignment is complicated by the fact that so many different body parts—the feet, knees, hips, shoulders, forearms, eyes—must be brought into position parallel to the target line. When you change just one of these factors, you exert some change on the desired ball flight. Pay attention to all alignments.

Corridor of Success for Spine Tilt (between 2° and 10° of right side bending at address).

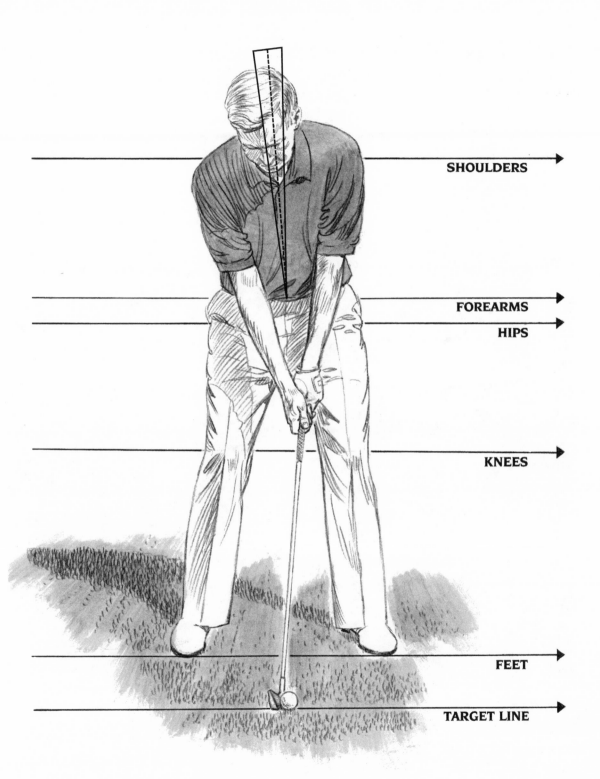

SHOULDERS

FOREARMS

HIPS

KNEES

FEET

TARGET LINE

SET UP TENSION FREE

Tension is often a by-product of poor concentration, but in the golf swing, tension threatens to undo all your preparations. *Tension kills the golf swing.* A quick check for signs of tension is to observe the forearms, wrists, hands, and thighs. If the muscles are contracted and tensed, your swing is in trouble before it begins. Back away, breath deeply and exhale very slowly, shake out the tension, then *reset* in a relaxed manner. Remember to evaluate your grip pressure on a scale of one (*super-light*) to ten (*super-tight*), and for normal shots, keep it right around five or under (*moderate to light*).

Address (left) and impact (right) are not the same.

THE SET UP POSITION DOES NOT SIMULATE IMPACT POSITION

I'm amazed at the number of students I teach who believe they strike the ball by returning the club to the same position they set at address. This is totally incorrect. To see the difference, thumb through some of your old golf magazines and view photographs of the pros at impact. The positions they are in do not look much like their set up positions, do they? What has happened is that everything has shifted toward the target. The weight is at least 70 percent to the left side. The hands are well out in front of the address alignment. The left wrist is flat. The right heel is off the ground and the right knee is kicking forward at the ball. The hips are turned well left, about thirty degrees. The shoulders should also be slightly open to the target line. Clearly, not much resembles the alignments made during the setup.

REVIEW

To the proficient pro, the preshot routine is *automatic*. However, by writing out all of these minute details, I run the risk of making this process appear tedious and perhaps overimportant to you amateurs. The fact is, you can have the greatest routine in the game but never reach your potential as a golfer if your swing technique is incorrect. With no golf game, a preshot routine is worthless.

Let me now give you an Eight-Step Swing "prep," so you will be better ready to learn and absorb the vital movements involved in a good swinging action.

PREPARING FOR THE EIGHT-STEP SWING

Before reading the next chapter on the Eight Steps, it's critical for you to know several truths about my teaching.

I don't teach the Eight-Step Swing all at once. Often, I do not even mention the steps in a particular order. Rather, as I analyze a swing, I mentally use these positions to organize my approach to each individual. It tremendously improves my ability to develop a game plan.

I then use these points in the swing to key in on problems. My teaching plan then becomes much easier for each individual lesson. My game plan is to diagnose the first problem in the player's swing. Once this is identified, I analyze why it is happening and then determine how I'll attack the problem.

The concept of swinging through eight steps is way too much for the average golfer. So, when I use the steps, I simply eliminate three or four positions. The key positions for the average player are Steps Two, Four, Six, and Eight. *These four steps should be clear in the golfer's mind.*

Many advanced players can easily adapt to all of the steps, if necessary. After an advanced player visualizes the steps and then carefully swings through all of the positions, it's only a matter of time until it becomes routine. Soon enough, there will be no thoughts in his or her mind about swinging into or through exact positions.

You need not attempt to master exact positions in golf. Nobody has a perfect swing. Trying to be perfect generally leads to overanalysis and a loss of freedom. Letting go, having freedom in your swing, is a huge key to golf success.

Placing the club through certain positions can, however, produce tremendous results. I believe that, to a significant degree, you can place the club into positions through the backswing. I sometimes have students think of the backswing as a "placement situation." If you know the locations, you can, in time, achieve dramatic results. The time required is different from player to player, but it can be achieved.

From technically correct backswing positioning (body plus club), the chances of achieving fundamental downswing and forward swing positions are greatly enhanced.

On the other hand, I believe that the move down to the ball (to impact) cannot be guided. Rather, you need to let go, to commit forward with abandonment. Think: *control back; let go forward!* Any top professional will tell you that to gain control of your shots you will need to give up control of your swing.

These eight steps are positions I have used in my teaching for many years. In fact they are the same eight fundamental steps I used in writing "The Ten Fundamentals of the Modern Golf Swing" (videotape) in 1987.

BACK TO SCHOOL

In our golf schools at Doral, we:

● Tell students how to swing. (You could also consider reading about this topic.)
● Show students, through pro demonstrations or video, the vital swing movements.
● Teach students "feel" by having the professional take hold of the club and move it into particular positions.
● Isolate a particular problem position of the swing and correct it by having the student perform a drill.

A FINAL WORD

Identify the areas of your swing that need work by watching your swing on video or through professional analysis. Follow my three-stage program for improvement:

1 Identify exactly what it is you are presently doing. This is where video is critically important. Clearly develop an accurate picture of your game.

2 After determining what you're doing at this time, determine what "exactly" is the movement (or swing action or change) that you want to do instead. (This is where the clarity of the Eight-Step Swing system accelerates the learning process.) I've noticed that most golfers go to the range not really knowing their swing or having a current picture of what they are doing. Furthermore, they don't really know what they are trying to do or change. As a result, they are susceptible to listening to anyone walking up and down the range. That might be another mid-high handicapper or a nonexperienced husband or wife. Everyone, as we all know, is a golf instructor.

3 Read a super golf book or seek out a qualified teacher to help you improve the mistakes that have been clearly identified and diagnosed. You need accurate feedback and information to make the changes. You need to know *how* to make the change.

THE EIGHT-STEP SWING
A NO-NONSENSE APPROACH TO CONSTRUCTING AN EASY-TO-REPEAT, PRO-TYPE SWING

STEP ONE: THE FIRST MOVE IN THE BACKSWING

FOR THE AVERAGE WEEKEND GOLFER

Watch the accomplished golfer make a smooth movement of the club away from the ball. Strive for a slow one-piece motion as you begin the take-away.

COMPLETE INSTRUCTIONS FOR THE ADVANCED PLAYER

The point in the backswing when the clubhead has moved about three feet away from the ball may seem like a premature time for evaluation. Not so at all. This is *Step One* in a solid golf swing, and I regard this initial move as fundamental. In fact, if you can master the requirements of Step One, the remainder of the swing will fall into place more easily. If Step One is flawed, the golf swing is in a state of recovery until impact. It is extremely important to be precise at Step One. It is the one area of the swing in which there is little room for personal preference. Strive for precision at Step One.

What starts the club back? Interestingly, it should be a mini move forward. You can take control of this vital initial movement by triggering it with a mini move of your own choosing. I suggest you lift your right heel slightly and return that heel to the ground as a trigger. Or use a slight body press toward the target. (I don't teach the forward hand press, because it activates the hands too much in the take-away.) With practice, this

Step One: Two views.

ignition move becomes totally second nature and is usually unnoticeable to the average golfer. This mini move forward helps create a beautiful rebound or counter–mini movement back to the right (weight shift). Therefore, the first move in the backswing is slightly forward.

Then comes the first move back, which should be a *one-piece* action. In other words, everything together—shoulders, arms, hands, hips, and legs. Weight distribution in the feet can be sensed early—you are off the left foot and onto the right. The left-foot–right-knee action is critical to a proper one-piece take-away. Sensation in the feet should be strongly felt, while the movement of the club should have an unforced, involuntary quality to it.

As the club first moves back, your head may move laterally a bit on any full swing. Although the head naturally moves, *both eyes* must remain on the ball. The head's slight lateral motion accommodates a rotation of your upper spine and weight shift onto your right leg. *Many great ball strikers have early lateral head motion.*

Early on, the *axis* of the swing has shifted to the inside of your right leg. The right leg becomes the backswing pivot point. *The right leg is the post you will turn on.* Think of your take-away as a miniature movement to the side far more than as a rotation around the center of your body. Golfers who think "turn" as they go to Step One are highly prone to employing a "reverse pivot," that is, loading weight onto the left foot instead of the right foot.

The clubshaft, meanwhile, stays between the arms. There is no conscious effort to guide the club. The clubface stays square to the arc of the swing with no conscious rotation. Grip pressure in each hand stays constant (at a moderate lightness).

The job of the hands is only to *maintain feel*. The arms, hands, and club are put into motion by the shoulders, the legs, and weight shift. There is a sensation that the club is swinging away freely, with no rigidity of the hands and arms. At the same time, control is maintained: you can feel exactly where the clubface is located and how it is oriented. In a natural swing action, which follows an arc, the clubhead rises up gradually along that arc. So be cautious not to overdo the dragging action of the club or to pick up the club abruptly with your hands. Top players use descriptive phrases like "sling the club back" and "pump it back with your left knee" to get across the idea that the hands and arms are, to this point, only along for the ride.

A proper weight shift in Step One moves your weight to the inside of the right foot and toward the right heel. It is critical that you maintain the flex in your right knee during this step. The right leg is your brace. It accepts the weight transfer and helps maintain your shoulders and hips at address levels.

If the big muscles of the body are used for the take-away, there will be no quick or jerky motions. Rather, the pace is slow and smooth, setting the stage for good tempo with every shot. Many times the only swing thought a great player will have is "smooth take-away."

If you have correctly established the right leg as the backswing support post, you can pivot with a "connected" one-piece action. You will be off to a smooth start. It is a take-away you can practice and perfect. It is a take-away you can repeat under pressure and is the first key to consistency. Remember, it's not your job or your responsibility to pull the club inside the target line as a conscious act. This inside tracking will take care of itself, but if and only if your take-away is proper. Through the Step One position, the club will, in fact, appear and feel too far outside the arc of the swing. Unless you push your left arm out and away, however, you'll never be outside; just stay connected.

BASIC GUIDELINES FOR THE WEEKEND PLAYER OR BEGINNER

- Use some slight motion to ignite your take-away. A small forward press of the legs and/or waggle of the club should work well. I recommend a lifting and replanting of the right heel. Whichever trigger mechanism you choose, practice it and stick with it. Start your swing with momentum.
- Take the clubhead away from the ball smoothly in a one-piece motion (shoulders, arms, hands, hips, and club start away together), making sure that your body stays level (does not dip or raise) and is free of any tension.
- When the clubhead is approximately three feet to the back of the ball, check to see if the clubshaft is still between your arms, weight has shifted onto the inside of your right leg, and that you have maintained the flex in the right knee.

NEGATIVES YOU MUST AVOID

1. Dipping or raising your head and body.
2. Tension in your arms and hands.
3. A fast move away from the ball (usually with the hands).
4. Weight staying left or shifting left.

STEP TWO: HALFWAY BACK

COMPLETE INSTRUCTIONS AND OBSERVATION

We have reached the halfway-back position when the clubshaft is parallel to the ground and the butt of the grip is pointed

Step Two: Two views and the
Step Two Corridor of Success.

approximately at the target. This is an important checkpoint, although there is room for personal preference at this point. It's interesting to note that, at this split second, *the clubhead is as far from the target as it will ever get*. The clubface is square to the arc of the swing, with the toe of the "head" basically pointing upward. (Depending on the spine angle of the player during the setup, the clubface may appear slightly closed or slightly downward—this is okay.)

At the Step Two position, when you're one-fourth of the way through the swing, nothing should be badly trailing or leading. The club, arms, and shoulders have stayed connected as a single unit. This is your backswing "package." At Step Two, everything has worked together.

Specifically, at this point you should have (1) shifted most of your weight onto your right foot; (2) retained the same degree of flex in your right knee as you started with at address (there will be a little "float" with the right knee, but not much);

(3) retained the flex in your left knee, with it broken inward and pointing behind the ball; (4) kept your right arm slightly above your left (in the manner of Lee Trevino) or well above your left (in the manner of Seve Ballesteros and Jack Nicklaus).

Death Move: if the right arm is visible *under* the left arm, you have committed a *Death Move,* caused by either rolling your forearms and the club far too much to the inside of the ball-to-target line or leaving your body center still, in an all-arms take-away. In either case, you have swung your arms incorrectly away from your body.

It is important to note that the clubface position at Step Two is not tightly mandated. Nor are you required to have the clubshaft pointed directly at the target. Some of the top ball strikers in the world vary on these points noticeably. Bruce Lietzke and Ray Floyd, for example, take the clubshaft inside at Step Two. In contrast, Fred Couples, Lee Trevino, and Curtis Strange take the shaft outside at Step Two. All five players, however, are able to correct their alignments during the down-swing, which is the essential key to ball-striking success.

Slight deviations from the so-called perfect alignments and positions of the clubshaft and clubhead at Step Two are not to be tinkered with, if indeed you are able naturally and smoothly to self-correct them in the downswing.

COMMON ERRORS AND POSSIBLE *DEATH POSITIONS*

1. *No hip turn and/or no weight shift*. This indicates that the legs were "dead" and the take-away was controlled too much with the arms.
2. *Locking of the right leg*. Overrotation of the hips or a reverse pivot accompanies this loss of knee flex.
3. *Rolling clubface open*. The clubface has fanned and rolled too far open. This is caused by overactive, independent wrist and arm action.
4. *Clubface in an extremely shut position*. This error is the result of a manipulation of the club with your hands or an exceptionally steep shoulder turn. If you assume a weak left-hand grip or reverse pivot, you're likely to shut the clubface.

⑤ *Excessive extension of the left arm.* This error is most often caused by the player who pays too much attention to the adage "Keep your left arm straight." The long left arm is actually an overextension from the shoulder. It is indicative of an early disconnection in your backswing.

⑥ *Right arm folding immediately into the body.* The high handicapper makes a conscious effort to hold his or right elbow against the body on the take-away. This is totally unnatural and it causes vital power to be lost.

STEP THREE: THREE-QUARTER BACKSWING POSITION

Step Three is reached when the backswing is approximately three-quarters complete. It is an excellent position at which to stop and view your action on videotape. Here's what to look for:

- Your left arm should be nearly parallel to the ground and reasonably straight, but not stiff. It should also be very close to being parallel to the ball-target line. If it is skewed on an angle that takes it way off the line, you're in serious trouble. This is a clear-cut disconnection of the swing. The right arm has pulled too far around.

- Because the wrist cock is nearly complete, the club and your left arm form an **L**. I believe that in this point in the swing *the club should feel light.* This is another point at which there is certainly room for personal preference. Some of the top players in the world cock their wrists quite early in the swing—such as Seve Ballesteros, Fuzzy Zoeller, and Nick Faldo. Others don't finish the wrist cock until later in their swings—for example, Greg Norman, Fred Couples, Davis Love, Curtis Strange, and Jack Nick-laus. However, at Step Three, most top players have cocked their wrists and formed the **L** angle.

- You should have maintained the same "knuckle count" as you established at address. Your left wrist should not roll or twist, which would add knuckles. Nor should the club curl under, which would subtract knuckles. Either of these wrist actions can cause the clubface to

Step Three: Two views.

close or open excessively off the plane of the swing.

- In a model swing, the left wrist is nearly flat—in line with your left forearm. And the face of the club should be pointed in line with your left wrist. We call this a "square clubface" position. Nice to have, but not critical, and certainly no "secret" to get overexcited about. Again, there is no one *perfect* position at the top.

- You should feel very balanced. *Note:* traveling from Step Three to the completion of the backswing is virtually a matter of momentum. A bit of wrist cock remains to be completed, but otherwise the impetus to return back to the ball is more or less dominant. From here we are set up just to carry on to the top, from which point the arms will free-fall back to the golf ball.

- Grip pressure should be equal in both hands. On my scale of one to ten, grip pressure is five or less. Duplicating the pressure established during the setup is a good goal. Maintain what you had at address.

- You should feel that your weight has shifted toward the right heel and slightly inside the right foot—but never toward the toes.
- Your right knee should have retained its flex. The left knee, of course, is far easier to keep flexed. By Step Three, it has moved to its maximum extension.

 *Death Move*: right knee lockup. Right knee lockup tends to accompany weight onto the toes and also onto the outside of the right foot (a common, but seldom noticed flaw). When golfers, particularly beginners, get stuck on this motion, they consign themselves to sloppiness in the leg action overall.

- Your chin should have rotated to the right and/or your head should have shifted slightly. If the head remains completely stationary, the pivot becomes rigid and nonathletic. There must be a slight rotation or shift of the head to the right. Please understand, I am talking about the movement of the head. The gaze of the eyes should not shift or wander; it remains casually focused on the golf ball.
- Ideally, you have not manipulated the clubface or your hands whatsoever through Step Three.

STEP FOUR: 100 PERCENT OF YOUR SHOULDER TURN (BACKSWING COMPLETED)

Step Four is marked by the completion of the back-around movement of the body and the club, just before the return move toward the target. At Step Four, the upper body has completed its windup and the uncoiling of the lower body has already begun. Yet, because the lower body initiates the downswing before the upper body finishes turning back, there is no defined end to one phase and beginning of the next phase.

Obviously, flexibility, stature, and physique of individual golfers give different looks and lengths to the full backswing position. That is why I say to make your personal 100 percent turn on a full shot. For some that translates to one hundred degrees; for others, seventy-five degrees. Therefore, there is no

one at-the-top position to emulate. Having said that, certain basics for employing a sound backswing always apply. Let me now summarize those universal elements and body positions, relative to Step Four.

Step Four: Two views.

SUMMARY FOR THE ADVANCED PLAYER

HIP/SHOULDER TURN POSITIONS

Throughout these step-by-step commentaries, the idea of connection is emphasized. All the same, at Step Four in the swing, the separation of the shoulders and hips is now complete. At this juncture in a full swing, your shoulders have rotated eighty to one hundred degrees and your hips have turned between forty and sixty degrees. This is just a model for simple numbers. Your left shoulder is behind the ball and close to being in line with the inside of your right leg. Of course, partial shots like a punched eight iron would follow a miniature version of this. For a general picture, the shoulders turn twice as much as the hips on most shots.

KNEE ACTION

Your left knee is pointed slightly behind the ball but is stable. Your left heel may be slightly off the ground for longer shots. It is okay for the heel to come off the ground if it is "pulled" off as a result of a proper pivot. Under no condition should it be consciously lifted. Meanwhile, your right knee has retained its flex and is stable. You shouldn't lose the flex in your right knee, or you'll give up all the good body lines you established at address. Your knees have turned approximately twenty-five degrees (see figure at right on page 78). At the top of the backswing, the lower body has already started back to the left. The knee turn is approximately 25 percent of the total shoulder turn and 50 percent of the hip turn.

WEIGHT SHIFT

Your weight should be toward the right heel and on top of the right foot. This is very important. If the weight goes to the outside of your right foot or toward the toes, balance is impaired.

FOOTWORK

Good footwork in the backswing is critical to good shot making. Therefore, you want to roll weight off the inside of your left foot. Ankle flexibility is needed for this rolling—practice it often. Also, connection of the left heel with the ground is important. On most shots, the left heel doesn't leave the ground. On longer shots, it should not rise more than an inch or so. Last, your footwork should be rhythmic. Thinking of the golf swing as a *dance step* will help you accomplish that goal.

HEAD AND CHIN POSITIONS

Your chin must rotate its maximum distance to the right by Step Four. In some players, this may be as much as forty-five degrees. The average rotation is twenty to twenty-five degrees. In addition, close scrutiny of hundreds of great players' swings on stop-action video shows there may be a lateral shift of the head of between one and four inches, or more. None of the great players freezes the head in the address position.

LEFT ARM POSITION

Your left arm may be slightly bent at the elbow. The key point is that it be firm but not stiff, rigid, and full of tension. Golfers have read and heard so much about a straight left arm, they tend consciously to stiffen it in an effort to avoid any bend.

HAND ACTION

Once you've completed your pivot, keep your hands *quiet*. Many players, hoping to gain distance by increasing the size of their swing arc, will continue to swing their arms and hands upward after the pivot is complete. In fact, this attempt to pick up club-head speed and add power to the swing almost always backfires. Overswinging the hands causes disconnection between the swing center and the club. The clubshaft gets thrown above the plane and, on the downswing, will usually cross over the ball-to-target line. This impairs flush impact and sets up the slice or any variety of weak shots.

WRIST POSITION

There is no precisely perfect wrist position at the top of the swing, no position that will guarantee a return of the clubhead to the ball in a completely square angle. Hand size, grip configuration, strength, and the degree of lateral motion during the downswing all influence clubface angle. Among top players, Tom Watson, John Mahaffey, Lee Trevino, Tom Weiskopf, and Bruce Lietzke tend to exhibit closed clubface angles at the top, while Ben Hogan, Curtis Strange, Jose-Maria Olazabal, and Johnny Miller, to name a few, have had the clubface open at the top.

Parameters of preference are allowed in clubface orientation at the top. I'm concerned only when the parameters are exceeded and the student exhibits a super-shut or super-open clubface at Step Four or when the student cannot square the clubface from his or her present top-of-the-swing position.

SHOULDER/ARM RELATIONSHIP

The arms swing in front of your body center. Even though momentum will carry the arms somewhat up and across the chest, a good swing thought is, "When the shoulders stop winding the arms, stop swinging."

STEP FOUR: DEATH MOVES

1. Even if you had yourself in good positions through Steps One, Two, and Three, you are at risk of tipping your body weight back to your left side, if you overturn your shoulders and arms at Step Four. That "little extra" you strive for at Step Four can lead to a legitimate *Death Move*. It is possible to overturn.

2. In a model natural swing, the clubface will always appear to open in the backswing, then close again through impact. Step Four should find it in a position that allows you to "get to impact square." If the clubface is turned drastically skyward (extremely closed) at this point in the swing, trouble awaits you. This position is almost impossible to recover from.

3. If you are wide open at the top, you'll tend to throw your hands at the ball through impact and hit a slice shot right of target. The wide-open position is very common to the high handicap player. So use video to check your at-the-top position.

Step Five: Front view and down target.

STEP FIVE: MOVE DOWN TO THE BALL

If there is a secret to employing a good golf swing, it occurs here.

In all the great swings I have studied, there is no evidence of a "stop" and "start" that together reverse the direction of the club from backswing to downswing. Instead, I see a smooth, flowing transition. The arms, hands, and club respond to the actions of the lower body. In fine golf swings, the last thing to change direction at the top is the clubhead. This, of course, makes perfect sense, because all the centrifugal and centripetal force we apply in the swing is designed to do nothing else but load the clubhead with energy and deliver it down the proper path.

In the transition, your arms and hands are passive. The first move is backward and down. The clubhead sinks lower as your hips start to unwind. Your hands and wrists respond to the reversal of direction. Your right elbow automatically drops into the proper slot by your right side. The Step Five checkpoint position in many ways resembles the Step Three position on the backswing. From a head-on view, it looks as if the hands and clubshaft were passing back through the same positions they were in at Step Three (only considerably narrower). There is a sense that the hands free-fall down to the delivery position (see the figure on page 22).

The right shoulder helps determine the path of the downswing. If, in its first motion, your right shoulder rocks down, all systems are go. Thanks to the shoulder, your right elbow can now drop into its proper slot and align (head-on view) with your right hip. This lowering of the right shoulder is a response to the legs' initiating the forward motion. But if the first motion is initiated by your right shoulder out toward the ball, you've got no chance to attain the correct positions at Step Five. This down tuck of the right shoulder can be overworked, so proceed with caution. You don't want to cause your left shoulder to "overclimb" through impact.

Note: to clear up any possible misconception, I have not said that the first move in the downswing is made by the right shoulder. The downswing starts with the hips or lower body moving toward the target. The shoulder motion, good or bad, is a responsive motion that ties in with the hips or lower body.

In a model swing, the hands and arms are passive during this step and respond to rather than initiate any action. The right elbow gives the appearance of attaching to, then being glued to, the right side just above the right hip area. The left arm is fully extended from the body—straight. It is here that good players feel pull, but that is only a sensation, not a result of any conscious manipulation with the hands or arms. With your right elbow glued to your right side and your left arm straight, it is easy to see that Step Five is a very connected position. Your hands and arms have not "run off" but are simply responding accurately and appropriately to the body motions. The clubshaft is very close to the same position it was in at Step Three—exceptions include ninety degrees of angle or more with the left arm. The downswing is inside (narrower than) the backswing. Your wrists are in a fully cocked position. The club should not be outside your hands. If it is, this is a perfect illustration of "casting" (starting the release motion too soon) or exaggerating the initial rotation of the shoulders. The "delivery position," as I call it, will always show you the golfer's impact position. It is a critical spot in the swing that determines all ball flight. It is always a position I carefully analyze in my teaching.

At Step Five, body weight has shifted back noticeably to the left. It has recentered the body and weight is shifting forward and *diagonally left*.

Your hips have slid seven to twelve inches toward the target, from Step Four to Step Six. This hip slide is a natural response to the lower body—the feet and legs—initiating the downswing. It happens *automatically* in a sequenced swing. If you monitor the belt buckle on any top player, you'll immediately see this powerful lateral movement.

At Step Five, the shaft should have fallen down along a path that, when viewed down the target line, is defined by the tip of your shoulder and your right elbow. If the shaft stays in this *Corridor of Success*, the butt end of the club points to an extension of the ball-to-target line, indicating an on-plane swing and promising solid contact and good trajectory.

In viewing the swings of the amateurs I teach, I sometimes see the shaft improperly low—dropped beneath the elbow. In this case, the dotted line from the shaft butt hits the ground at a point well beyond the target line. From this position you will push or hook the ball—if you make solid contact. Often, you will hit behind the ball from this inside, shallow swing arc.

A far more common problem I witness is indicated when the shaft moves downward on a path that takes it above the tip of the shoulder. In this instance, a line drawn from the butt of the club would point to the player's feet. We call this "shaft tip over." From this position at Step Five, you will usually contact the ball with the toe of the clubface and hit a weak slice. A *Death Position*! If you manage to square the clubface, you'll pull the ball. Finally, this move is also characteristic of the shank.

STEP FIVE: FINAL CHECKPOINTS

1. The right knee has kicked forward (toward the ball or target line), and there is a substantial space between your knees.
2. The hips have shifted a few inches, in response to your weight-shifting action, and reached the square position. The shoulders trail the hips.
3. The head has stabilized at, or slightly behind, its address position.

④ The right heel is grounded or, at most, slightly off the ground. At this point in the swing, it should never be extra high.

⑤ The flexed left knee is forward of your left hip. The left knee is more or less in a straight line with the middle of your left foot. The left leg is still flexed but is in the process of straightening.

⑥ The body has entered the classic "sit-down" position many players and teachers have long observed (below).

⑦ The clubshaft is on plane.

⑧ The shoulders are unwinding at a rapid pace, yet still lag your hips in rotation. The golf swing depends heavily on "connection," but in the downswing we also see two instances of *separation*—first, the lower body "leaves" the shoulders, then the hands and arms "separate" from the shoulders. The distance between your hands and right shoulder increases as the club reaches our "delivery position."

⑨ The right arm should be slightly visible under your left starting down.

⑩ Your eyes are fixed on the ball.

⑪ The clubhead is behind your body.

⑫ Many golfers will benefit by *slowing down* the turn back to the target. Sometimes it is useful to slow the upper torso—other times the lower—and sometimes both.

⑬ A big secret to good shot making is the clubshaft position at Step Five and the square orientation of the clubface. I call this "the delivery position."

THE SIT DOWN (FOR ADVANCED PLAYERS ONLY)

All powerful throwing motions proceed in a sequence of weight shift, rotation, arm swing—or "shift-rotate-throw." In all such acts, the quality of the sequence affects final impact speed tremendously. In the golf swing, "sitting down" at the right time recenters weight just as the swing's most dramatic and important weight transfer is about to take place. (The start of the downswing.)

The sit down is subtle, but feeling your left knee move back toward the target in a *half-circle motion*, feeling your right knee

STEP FIVE: DEATH MOVES

1. The clubshaft is "tipped over" or above your right shoulder, or the clubshaft is directly above your hands.

2. The clubshaft has dropped under your right elbow and is parallel to the ground (or almost parallel); your right palm faces the sky.

3. The head is facing toward the target or your eyes have moved off the ball.

4. The body slides or drifts too far past the ball. This is caused by your weight sliding left too early. It is most visible in the upper body. When the legs go dead, the upper body will usually slide ahead.

5. The clubface is extremely open or closed.

kicking at the golf ball, feeling a *push* off your right instep, or feeling your left hip start its *rotation* back toward the target will allow you to understand it better. It can also be felt as a split-second recentering of the body before the full power rotation into impact, and beyond. *At this position, a good checkpoint is to see if your thighs and knees are parallel to the target line.*

The sit down can be encouraged and practiced, but it does not occur at a static, isolated moment, such that it can be attended to before the golfer moves on to striking the golf ball. It is simply a position you *move through* in the golf swing. It is also something you must practice to help your body understand the correct movements. The continued rotation of the hips, the firing of the right side, the commitment forward to the finish position automatically straightens up the braced left side of the body. The left leg will be straight or nearly straight at impact. From sit down, we will move toward *stand up*. This is natural and will happen automatically with correct hip action.

The sit down is a big key to hitting the ball powerfully. To master it, think *lower body resistance and then lower body initiation*. Practice a right arm (sidearm) throwing motion, such as you would use to skip a flat rock across a pond or lake. Last, constantly examine your swing in a mirror. Make normal and slow-motion swings without a club to get your body actions into correct sequence. Make some incorrect motions on purpose, then compare the feel of them with the proper motion. You will most likely need to consult the services of a PGA teaching professional to get this absolutely right. If done correctly, this motion tremendously helps put the arms and club into our perfect "delivery position."

Warning: as the change of direction is initiated via the lower body, the hands, wrists, and arms are passive. A likely cause of missing the sit-down motion is that your hands, wrists, and arms become active, without your lower body moving. The result: the throw is preceding the shift and the rotation. *When sequence is destroyed, loss of power and off-center hits ensue.*

A related problem is the initiation of the downswing with the upper body, the shoulders in particular. Results: your hands are thrown much too far outward, the club does not fall in, and the downswing is too steep and too out-to-in.

STEP SIX: IMPACT

At last: the *moment of truth*. If you consistently arrive at the impact position with the proper alignments and sufficient club-head speed, whatever your swing looked like getting there is irrelevant. Whatever small mistakes and swing flaws you committed along the way are forgiven.

Any player who can arrive at an excellent impact position consistently with speed has what we all strive so hard to achieve: a repeating (therefore, *perfect*) swing—for that player. The look of a swing is, in the final analysis, overrated. Why else would we see so many champion golfers with highly individualized swing characteristics? The most important characteristic they share is this: they all arrive in the impact position with the same solid consistency.

Step Six: Two views.

I have spent long hours minutely comparing the swing of top players and have come to this conclusion: any accomplished player, including such unconventional swingers as Lanny Wadkins, Bruce Lietzke, Lee Trevino, and Miller Barber, stretch the parameters of preference to the outer limits. But would they have been better players following some "perfect model"? I think not. We probably would never have heard of them. That natural brilliance of a gifted athlete should not be removed if he or she consistently gets to Step Six. Ironically, at Step Six—impact—these players all look amazingly alike. Differences fall away and common points abound. For example, each clubface is square, each player's angle of attack is on plane, the ball contact is on the center of the clubface, and the clubhead speeds are all high. And the left and right hands of these players are working as a tight unit, not fighting each other. By the way, a wonderful sensation to feel at impact is that of the right side "firing" fully and the clubface *covering the ball*. Jimmy Ballard has long used this phrase to express the feeling you get when contact is flush and the clubhead and ball seem to be united along the target line for an extra split second.

Here are some vital facts about impact:

- The left wrist must be flat or slightly arched (or bowed, or supinated) at Step Six. The worst power loss you can experience is the inward collapsing of the left wrist at impact. Common causes of this power loss are a slowing down of the hands through impact—which happens when a player attempts to steer the clubhead into the back of the ball—or overacceleration of the clubhead—in which the right hand causes the clubhead to run out ahead of the hands before impact. In a still photograph, you would see that overacceleration causes the clubshaft to line up with the right arm rather than the left arm, as it should. Both conditions result in a great loss of power. They are not often discussed, but these two swing malfunctions are terribly common among high-handicap golfers.
- The right wrist must be angled at impact, not straight, to match up with the flat left wrist. The angle of the right wrist is one of the very few characteristics that replay the look of the address position. Therefore, the right wrist must not hinge forward. The hands and wrists must work together throughout the swing, and they can't if the right wrist hinges independently.
- The left arm and clubshaft, when viewed from above, should line up with each other. The shaft cannot lag too far behind the left arm, nor can it pass the left arm before impact. Both of these conditions indicate serious mistiming of the swing.
- Weight has transferred to the left leg and is on the left foot, more toward the heel. The right heel is one to four

inches off the ground; some players will feel a push off the right foot—an excellent key, by the way.

- The right knee has fired forward at Step Six, up to about your body centerline. An effective timing key is to think, "Right knee and hands back to the ball together." The left knee will still have a slight flex to it. The legs are spaced apart from one another, rather than having the right leg passing over and catching the left; if this happens, the probable cause is too narrow a stance, too much hip action, or overly fast feet and leg action.
- There is space between the legs.
- The right elbow is very close to the right hip and still shows a slight bow.
- The right heel is ahead of the right toe.
- The chin has returned to its starting position or is now pointing toward the ball. (On wood shots, the head may be slightly behind where it started.)
- The hips and shoulders have maintained some spacing and a degree of separation. In other words, the hips are leading the shoulders and the shoulders must not catch up to the hips. What the hips have done is clear well to the left (about thirty degrees) as a result of proper rotation. The shoulders will also be slightly left at impact, ten to twenty degrees. *Remember:* it is far easier to slide the hips toward the target than it is to rotate them clear to the left—don't get sloppy and just "hip slide" forward.
- The body stands up a little bit at impact. That's because we are using the ground as leverage to get power into the swing.
- The right elbow is still slightly bent at impact. It is only after impact that the right arm fully straightens.

Before I move on to Step Seven, a note on head movement is called for here. Some golfers' heads, at the time of impact of club and ball, will have moved rearward and slightly behind their original address positions. Unquestionably, the head moves during the golf swing. Trying to freeze your head in one

During the downswing, many beginners have a tendency to employ the *Death Move* of swinging the right arm out and away from the body. In effect, the typical novice throws the clubhead at the ball.

Because impact occurs in an instant (0.0004 second), it may seem odd to devote great attention to it. Indeed, some students find it difficult to think about impact. Yet, I've found that working back from the perfect alignments of impact is an excellent teaching technique. Visualizing a perfect impact position and making lots of practice swings that stop at impact helps you feel the sensation of a good impact position.

TAKE THE TRIANGLE TEST

As a drill, practice retaining the important connections of your swing by checking the distance between the butt of the club and your navel. See that this gap does not decrease from impact through Step Seven.

Another important check involves the orientation of the club handle within the all-important triangle formed by your arms and your shoulder line. The club should remain in the center of the triangle through this phase of the swing. It should be like a spoke of a wheel, with the center of your abdomen acting as the hub. When the great Roberto de Vicenzo told me he "hit the ball with his stomach," it allowed me to appreciate the idea of proper *connection* through impact.

location can be a poor idea. *Typically, the head moves forward because your legs don't.* When you succeed in locking your head into position throughout the swing, you generally create trouble for yourself in other areas. The head reacts very naturally to the forces built up as a result of the motion and turning of the body. To attempt to restrict it completely is counterproductive. So, allow your head its natural motion—just keep your eyes focused on the ball until impact.

STEP SEVEN: EARLY FOLLOW-THROUGH

Step Seven of the golf swing is the segment between impact and the point at which your right arm is parallel to the ground. Some of the poor positioning and mistakes that occur at this point are the outgrowth of much earlier errors and problems, but other Step Seven mistakes crop up during and right after impact. The most notable problems at this stage tend to stem from a breakdown of the connection between the left shoulder and the left side of the chest. *This is perhaps the most important connection point of the swing,* and letting it break apart leads to two major flaws:

- The hands and the club overextend down the target line, the left arm disconnects from the left side, and the left wrist breaks down completely. When this happens, the left shoulder remains in view (to a face-on observer) long past the point at which it should no longer be visible. A hook, push, or flyer shot usually results.
- The left elbow slides across the body in a sawing motion; in a face-on view, the left shoulder disappears from view prematurely, the left arm breaks down, the left elbow points up toward the sky.

Thanks to the symmetry that is inherent in a sound golf swing, certain aspects of a proper Step Seven will mirror the good things seen in Step Five. For example, a good player's elbows and forearms will be nearly level to one another at this

Step Seven: Two views. Notice that you see no arms and no club in the photo on the right.

juncture, just as they were at the equivalent point of the down-swing. (Here you can lay a yardstick or a golf club across your forearms to test for levelness.) Slightly further in the follow through, an imaginary beam of light emanating from the butt end of the shaft will point directly at the ball-to-target line during the follow-through, just as it did at a corresponding phase of the downswing.

Looking up the target line at the golfer as he or she com-pletes Step Seven, you should observe that the line of the club-shaft extends out from the line of the right arm with only a slight angle at the hands. I've noticed the good player's club-shaft makes an unbroken straight line with his or her right arm, just past this checkpoint position. Moreover, the continuing rotation of the hips and body center through impact allows the golfer to remain connected through Step Seven.

This is also a point in the swing at which good footwork and legwork can sometimes bog down. Keep your legs and feet dri-ving off the earth and with your body weight moving to its even-tual point of total transfer to the left post, or left pivotal point of the swing (your left leg). The right heel is well off the ground.

If you are concerned that the full body action of your golf swing is insufficient, you should work on the full-swing turn-back-and-through motions with your arms crossed over your chest.

In doing this drill, focus on your right hip pocket (RHP) and your left hip pocket (LHP). The fact is, at the finish, you have to get your right pocket to the spot where your left pocket was at address. Drill this RHP motion whenever you get a chance.

NEGATIVES TO AVOID

LEFT SHOULDER CLIMB

Keep your shoulders level and turning on your spine tilt. In other words, avoid the classic "rock and block."

EYES GLUED TOO LONG TO THE SPOT

Once the ball is struck, you have no reason to keep focusing on the divot or tee; in fact, you will contribute to a breakdown of your overall swing if you don't allow your head and eyes to follow the ball once it is away. Ideally, the club is moving at a high rate of speed through impact. Trying to stay down too long will eventually cause you to experience back problems.

LEGS GONE DEAD AS FOLLOW-THROUGH BEGINS

Impact does not mean the legs have completed their task. Keep the weight moving and your footwork and legwork active. Keep your center, or your belt-buckle area, moving. This rotation through impact is very important. Facing the ball too long will disconnect the arms and promote incorrect body action.

STEP EIGHT: FINISH AND REBOUND

In the final phase of the swing, your momentum takes you to a completed follow-through position. Your hips and shoulders are fully rotated and the club is behind your head momentarily, before it returns to a relaxed, balanced position in front of your body. From this position, you just watch the ball travel to its landing area. The return of the club from behind your head is called a *rebound* or reflex action. This is the area I call "hit and evaluate." When you hit, hold, and evaluate your shot, you are accomplishing three important things: optimum *balance*, optimum *feedback*, and optimum *feel*.

Because all the motion of the swing is over, the finish and rebound are fairly easy aspects of your own swing to establish and evaluate. In a mirror, you should see, for example, that your right shoulder finished closer to your target than your left shoulder. And, as you return the club to a waist-high position on the rebound, you should feel that your grip pressure there, as well as at the finish, is no weaker than it was at impact. You haven't lost anything off your grip pressure, in other words. Your basic grip/hand position from address is the same.

If you are looking in a mirror that is pointed at you from the target area, you should notice that the clubshaft crosses through your head at the full-finish position. Its plane may well match the plane of your shoulders. I don't like to see the club flopped vertically over your shoulders like a heavy laundry bag.

During the downswing, weight travels across your feet in a rolling action. The front foot holds its basic position, as a brace against the force of the body, arms, and club as you contact the ball. If you spin your front foot from its original orientation—so that it ends up more or less parallel with the target line—your swing will be out of control and you'll lose power. This counter-clockwise turning of the left foot after impact is usually a compensation for poor balance earlier in the swing and indicates a spinout. Ironically, this unorthodox "foot fault" will help you regain balance as you move to the top of the finish, but the spinout is a bad sign. No top player makes this move. If anything, great players—Jack Nicklaus and Greg Norman, for example—may actually move their left heel forward, toward the target on the downswing, to brace themselves further and to provide a force to "hit against."

By making a balanced, athletic swing and holding your connections together, you can hit a big golf shot and finish at an exact stop without forcing it. Many great players practice by swinging full and holding their finishes like statues. Normally, the only time you will see a tour pro incapable of holding his or her finish is when he or she has made a hard swing from a dramatically uneven lie, such as on the wall of a bunker. But the poor player shows this fidgety, teetering finish on shots from flat ground. Avoid this and be conscious of balance.

OPPOSITE
Step Eight: Finish (top) and rebound (bottom).

1. There is one swing tip that will be your personal "secret" and you will never be able to overemphasize it.

2. You should play every shot off your left heel.

3. Place your weight out toward your toes at address.

4. Your arms should hang straight down from your shoulders when you set up.

5. All good players have good grips.

6. Barely grasp the club with your right hand.

7. Keep your head up at address.

8. Keep your head down throughout the motion.

9. Keep your left arm straight.

10. When your wrists are cocked at the halfway point of the backswing, the butt of the club should point at the ball.

11. A closed clubface at the top of the backswing automatically leads to hooking.

12. Pull the club down to the ball with your left arm.

13. Your head is the axis point of the swing, and it should stay still throughout the swing.

14. The right hand or right arm causes hooking.

15. Swing the club down the target line.

16. Finish high.

IN THE GROOVE
HOW TO MASTER
THE EIGHT-STEP SWING

Mention the word *practice* and most golfers picture driving ranges, blistered hands, sore muscles, and in recognition of this suffering, a small dose of success. No teaching professional, least of all this one, will deny the value of practicing correctly on the driving range. But hitting balls at the range is only part of the answer. Former Masters winner Claude Harmon figured this out long ago and would lament often about frustrated golfers trying to improve by mindlessly "beating balls" on the range.

Claude would tell a story about a man who buys a new two hundred thousand dollar Ferrari, jumps in his car, then leaves Winged Foot Golf Club (in Westchester County, New York, where Claude taught) headed for New York City. He's on I-95, but mistakenly heads north instead of south. He puts the pedal to the floorboard and races down the highway at top speed, 180 miles per hour. He's making great time, but he's got two serious problems: he's getting farther from New York City with every mile and he's liable to kill himself in the process. Like the golfer beating balls with no clue, Claude would say, the man in the Ferrari has no direction, and sadly he will never reach his destination.

For some, too much practice on the range may actually impede progress. I have spent half my life on the practice range, and I promise you, there are more than a few golfers who hit balls on the range hour upon hour, day after day, and gain little if any benefit from their efforts. "More is better" does not always apply to practicing golf. The secret is to devote your time, whether it's a minute or several hours, to *practical practice*.

Correct golf movements might begin in the intellect, but they must end in the muscles, and muscle memory is cultivated through practice. People with superior physical aptitude will learn faster, but there is no one who becomes an excellent golfer without paying the price on "the rock pile." For a fundamental change to occur in your swing, there must be sufficient time for the conscious and unconscious mind to accept it. My rule of thumb is to allow about one month of steady effort for the student to internalize one significant component of a swing change. Then he or she can go on to the next new move.

The player who works consistently on solid fundamentals and makes progress in small segments will tend not to lose overnight what he or she has gained over time. When the player does slide backward, the slide will be minor and the turnaround not long in the making. There are no shortcuts to the mastery of golf; intelligent practice is the only way to narrow the gap between knowing something about the swing and employing it correctly.

I like to believe I have helped some players simply by changing their entire outlook on practice. Practice doesn't have to be just hitting balls down a driving range. It can be fun. It can be in short sessions. It can take place at home or in your backyard, and it can be greatly enhanced if you adopt a positive attitude toward the game and read helpful books and articles and study videotapes.

One interesting example along these lines occurred with Gary Player at my former Learning Center at Sleepy Hollow. During a practice session, I brought Gary inside to watch some particular video footage of Ben Hogan. It is some awesome footage of two specific swings that I knew Gary would love to see. Sure enough, he was tremendously interested. I replayed each swing hundreds of times, and we viewed the tape for more than two hours. Gary spent a great deal of time talking about what he saw and knew about Hogan.

After this in-depth viewing, Gary went back to the practice tee with more enthusiasm and a vivid picture of what he wanted to do. The next day he shot sixty-six in our Senior Tour event. Full credit went to those beautiful pictures of Hogan that stayed clearly in Gary's mind. I know, because he told me that the tape gave him a completely new feel and picture of what he was trying to do.

You are practicing whenever you are repeating exercises and drills on a regular basis, no matter where you happen to be. Golfers who are retooling their full swings often wonder if they can improve by taking one or two lessons or whether they need a six- or eight-week series. The number of formal lessons you take can be reduced significantly if you and your instructor can devise a detailed, comprehensive practice program that, incidentally, *will* involve doing swing drills without hitting balls.

Practicing with a weighted "donut" on your club helps you groove a good swing. Here holding the correct delivery position.

Practice the Eight-Step Swing using a regular club, swing fan, or a weighted club. It is very helpful to swing in front of a mirror. Put yourself in the correct positions (the positions you need to improve) and hold each one—over and over, the more repetitions the better. The more you practice in this way, the quicker your old habits and your old swing problems will melt away. Realize that changing a physical habit requires constant attention and repetition.

When you are on the range hitting balls, always execute a significant number of your shots using your full preshot routine. At least 20 percent of your shots on the range should be hit following a full implementation of your preshot pattern. This is practicing as you would play. It adds a whole dimension to practice. Try to hit two of every ten shots using a target and a preshot routine. This way, your practice will at least somewhat *simulate* actual play.

To enjoy golf to the fullest, you have to learn to enjoy the journey, with all its peaks and valleys and its occasional long plateaus. Reaching the final lofty destination takes a long time and focused attention on practicing the correct movements. It is not the destination, however, that is always most important. Instead, it is the striving and the paths you choose that provide the fun of golf. On some lucky days, you'll even feel that you are zipping along in a new Ferrari—headed in the absolutely correct direction, too.

Hitting to a target during practice will allow you to simulate the course situation.

GOOD AND BAD PRACTICE SWINGS

Ever heard someone say, "My practice swing is great, but when I go to hit the ball my swing is terrible"? We've all heard that statement groaned a thousand times. Has it ever struck you as somewhat illogical? If not, it should.

It isn't so much that the person's swing at the ball is so poor as it's the practice swing that is far less than he or she thinks it is. Usually the poor golfer has far overrated his or her practice swing. Most people have the same body movements and swing mistakes in their practice swing as in their real swing. What changes is their *tempo* and the fact that they are not impacting an object. Because they swing slowly with no fear of mishitting the ball, their practice swing feels pretty good. Only it isn't. The same mistakes that plague the real swing are there in the practice swing all along.

Practice swings are like push-ups. One push-up does nothing—but hundreds of push-ups done on a regular basis have a dramatic effect. Your practice swings are governed by a similar dynamic of repetition. Done correctly, the practice swing will eventually produce dramatic improvements. Done haphazardly—perhaps instilling *Death Moves*—the practice swing will only make improvement that much more elusive.

THE VALUE OF PRACTICE SWINGS AND DRILLS

I teach students from every walk and way of life. Golf has a varying degree of importance to each. There is no way for me, or any other instructor, to come up with a single practice schedule that will fit all golfers. There are too many variables. One breakthrough I have experienced with a broad range of students is to get them to appreciate the value of swinging the club or working on body motions. I encourage them to take practice swings at home, in the office, or in any setting where they can find just a few minutes. Getting them to make practice swings from a proper set to a proper follow-through for brief sessions has brought about significant swing improvements for many. Consistent, short practice sessions are usually much more beneficial than sporadic long sessions. This focused consistent approach speeds improvement. Significantly!

Equally important is the use of drills. Athletes in all sports work on drills to perfect their body actions and tune their muscles. Golf has lagged far behind other sports in this regard. To get better faster, by all means use appropriate drills.

Whenever I teach a particular position of the Eight-Step Swing, I find that drills are highly effective. Students quickly learn what they look like when correctly executing each position, and they learn how to arrive at each position. Students also understand that for each position there is an acceptable variance. In other words, there is usually room for a different look. This point is vital. When changing a position in your swing it's extremely helpful to view your swing constantly in a mirror (or watch it on videotape); it is important that you learn how to look at a golf swing and why good swings don't all look the same. The main reason they look different is that body size, physique, rhythm, tempo, and backswing locations differ so markedly from player to player. Picture the swings of these golfers: Miller Barber, Curtis Strange, Ben Hogan, Jack Nicklaus, David Frost, Nick Price, Jeff Sluman, and Nancy Lopez. Obviously, they are not carbon copies of each other, despite the fact that in their own ways, each player achieves the basic fundamental positions.

Now picture these players facing you in a police lineup. Considering how different they are in basic physique (not to mention the differences in metabolism, muscle tissue, and other internal systems), is it any surprise that their golf swings don't look alike on the surface? It should not be a surprise at all. The more you learn what to look for, however, the more the *similarities* will appear to you.

How to Know You Are Making Progress

Can you do it? Can you make a significant swing change or swing adjustment? The answer depends on your determination more than any other factor, but I believe it will be yes. By working with a qualified PGA teaching professional who will help keep you motivated and spot mistakes, most golfers can achieve their own acceptable version of the efficient, powerful golf swing shown in the Eight Steps. You'll know you are within reach of a consistent, fundamentally correct swing action when you can automatically go through the step or steps you have changed with no mechanical thought. Again, practice must be a constant, everyday activity. Even devoting a few minutes a day to practical practice will make a tremendous difference.

The "Feel" Side: Timing and Balance

Like all physical gifts, natural balance and fluid rhythm are not parceled out evenly to everyone. Yet they are probably the most important attributes of the athlete. Some players will never achieve that wonderful, graceful ease of motion that has made Sam Snead, Al Geiberger, Bruce Lietzke, Fred Couples, Phil Mickelson, Dottie Mochrie, Meg Mallon, and Brandie Burton so fun to watch. But you can still work toward improving your rhythm and balance. Physical conditioning and flexibility are factors in the achievement of fluid, even-tempo motion.

To improve your balance, rhythm, and tempo further, you should watch and imitate athletes who embody it. Whenever you can watch a top tour player, make sure to do so with an eye toward recording his or her tempo and storing the "tape" in some corner of your mind. When you get back home, let your body sense that same rhythm. This is the best way to smooth out your swing and keep it from being rigid, nonathletic, and mechanical. Sometimes, imitation—the old monkey-see, monkey-do—is the best way to learn. When you practice your swing, work hard on the coordination of your body parts. Focus on timing the club, arms, and body evenly. Sense a balance of all your parts and simplify your motion by using a 1-2-3-4 count or repeating a tune inside your head.

THE THEORY OF ELIMINATION

The more an instructor can break down the movement of the body and the club into separate elements, the clearer the student's understanding of the Eight-Step Swing. Furthermore, through repetition of isolated movements, it's possible to accelerate the learning process.

Here are some simple ideas I have long preached on the general topic of "elimination and isolation for improvement." Follow this system in sequence, and you'll quickly break down any learning impairments that have previously blocked you from reaching your true golfing potential. It has worked well for me.

1. *Eliminate the Course.* Take away the course. Get away from playing golf on the course. Instead, go to the driving range and concentrate on swing tempo and swing position improvements (relative to the Eight Steps). Going to

All good players pay their dues at the range. This is the place to work on mechanics where you can hit ball after ball.

Hitting into a net takes the anxiety of where the ball goes away. This can be very productive when making a swing change.

the range is a major stress reducer. Your golf muscles will be less tense, thereby enabling you to swing better.

2 *Eliminate the Range.* Take away the range. If you're not getting good results on the range, practice hitting balls into a driving net. This effectively eliminates ball flight anxiety. Without this deterrent, you will focus much more on the swing.

3 *Eliminate the Hit.* Take away the ball. In other words, focus solely on the swing. Now that the "hit impulse" is removed, you'll stop trying too hard and swinging too fast.

4 *Eliminate Bad Swings.* Take away the club. That leaves just the arms, legs, and body to do the swinging. Without the club, body awareness further improves.

5 *Eliminate Bad Motion.* Take away the arms. Fold your arms onto your chest and work on just footwork and body motion.

I simply keep "eliminating" until the student makes improved movements and understands exactly what should be done. Once accomplished, we move on.

Many times a clear picture of the swing will allow you to eliminate any unnecessary actions in your technique. So, if you and your instructor can isolate any faulty movements and work together to groove only those choice Steps that fall between the *Corridors of Success,* you will soon evolve into a very efficient swinger. Once you accomplish that goal, you are on your way to being a true "player." You'll have a dependable swing that you can produce under pressure.

PROBLEMS WITH POSITIONS

Teaching the swing through steps or positions is not new, as I've already emphasized. My Eight Steps or checkpoint positions are different because of the parameters, or *Corridors of Success,* that I believe allow for necessary individualism.

Systems that tightly standardize the golf swing are dangerous because few golfers can perform all the movements and swing positions of the model. System teachers who use rigid guidelines close their minds and eyes to other swing actions and body movements that can and, in fact, do work.

Hitting "every" shot according to a set system for swinging the club makes playing under pressure tremendously more difficult. My own shortcomings in this area led me to understand that many things can be overdone, some of the oldest accepted axioms were incorrect, and some teaching adages such as "hit late" had to be reevaluated.

At an early stage of development, especially with youngsters, staying steady and delaying the hit can be taught very successfully. However, using the arms and hands to create lag is usually only a stage of development. At a later, advanced stage, remaining motionless, staying absolutely centered (the stationary post), and continuously working on lag not only can become dangerous but can promote *Death Positions.*

This one example shows that some positions, when practiced to an extreme, can cause tremendous damage even to highly skilled athletes and, in the end, make the game much harder indeed.

Position instruction, breaking the swing into component parts, or teaching through steps is a tremendous accelerator to the learning process. Teaching this way is especially good for isolating problems and correcting the fault. Yet positions have limitations.

When swing mechanics become the entire focal point of the teacher, the student ceases to become a skilled player. Instead, he or she becomes a confused, tense, robotic golfer.

When a certain position or set of positions become the goal, the act of swinging and being an athlete often get lost in the details. We need to remember that a true swinging action produces the consistency we all desire. I maintain that *Corridors of Success* allow individual differences and individual talent to exist within the Eight Steps. This freedom will allow extremely talented golfers to do it "their way."

Remember that wherever you learn golf, including from me, ideas or fundamentals are based on what we have seen, learned, or experienced. Science tells us that today's laws of physics may be proven wrong tomorrow. So there is no system that may not be improved down the road.

In my opinion and my experience, teaching through a series of steps has exceptional instructional value. Yet these steps, or positions, have limitations. To quote Harvey Penick, "Take some of the medicine, but don't swallow the whole bottle."

Finally, I always emphasize what I call the "25 Percent Theory." This is the idea that golf is composed of four basically equal parts:

1. The long game
2. The short game
3. The mental game
4. The management game

LOOK AND LEARN
WATCHING THE PROS PLAY GOLF ON TV CAN TEACH YOU HOW TO THINK YOUR WAY TO LOWER SCORES

One way to improve your game is to observe the experts playing golf on television. In this chapter I will give you my ideas on what to look for when viewing a tournament, then tell you how to apply my "television guide" to your game. However, I'm not going to mention the elements of the swing or any specific shot-making keys you should observe. Much of what I'm about to relate concerns the abstracts of golf—those little things that taken individually make little, if any, difference but when tied together make the difference between winning or losing your match with the course or opponent.

Let's first look at the broad spectrum of course management. To illustrate a few things I've noticed on television, dial in the 1990 Masters. Raymond Floyd is leading the field and Nick Faldo by three shots after three rounds. Floyd is playing flawless golf. He is a two-time past Masters champion, who just so happens to be one of the greatest front-runners ever.

Faldo begins the fourth round with a big fat six, a double bogey. Yet, he does not panic, nor does he change any part of his pretournament game plan. He does not give up, though he has dropped to five shots behind Floyd.

Miraculously, Faldo fights back to within one shot of the lead as he stands on the eighteenth tee, his seventy-second hole. He knows that Floyd has made almost no bogeys for seventy holes. He can see that Floyd has only a short-iron or wedge shot approach to the seventeenth green.

What can Faldo be thinking as he plans his final tee shot up the famous eighteenth hole at Augusta? Put yourself in his shoes. Know this: a long perfect drive by Faldo could reach a flat area of the uphill undulating fairway. Definitely a big advantage. However, on the first three days of playing this hole, Faldo hit a three wood off the tee. The reason is simple. Faldo knows that this is his best play. Although a three wood will leave Faldo a long-medium–iron approach shot into the green off an uphill lie, it provides him the best chance to drive the ball in the fairway.

Now, what will he do—go with the three wood as he had planned or take a bit of a chance and nail the driver up to an area where he can hit a shorter iron from a more level spot? What would you do if you had the same swing skills as Faldo?

I don't believe Faldo ever considered the driver. He continued to follow his game plan, and *no* one professional golfer executes a game plan better than he does. He had determined the best way to play the final hole during his practice rounds, and he was going to stick to his strategy—no matter what! Even though Floyd looked unshakeable and it looked highly unlikely that he would bogey either of his last two holes, Faldo opted for the safer three wood. Did he feel this was aggressive golf? To him, yes. The reason: it had to be that Faldo felt that hitting the three wood would give him a shot from the fairway, while a slight mistake with the driver would eliminate a reasonable chance for scoring birdie three on the hole. Plus Faldo knew that no matter how talented a golfer is and no matter what kind of a roll he or she is on, that golfer is not exempt from hitting a poor shot or getting a bad break—especially when under severe pressure.

So, Faldo drives off the seventy-second hole with a three wood and must come into the green with a four iron off a significant upslope; most certainly not the easiest way to make birdie. Yet there Faldo is—in the fairway with a chance.

Somehow Floyd hits an uncharacteristic nine iron approach to the seventeenth green. Leaving himself an extremely difficult putt of around fifty feet, he three putts. Unexpectedly, Faldo and Floyd are tied.

At this point in the event, it is extremely interesting to study the two players. I listen carefully to certain commentators who have great knowledge of the game and who I believe give an honest appraisal of what is occurring. I totally disregard the commentary of other announcers who have little knowledge of tournament golf or who are more interested in hyping the situation or creating controversy than just stating the facts. The best commentators, Ken Venturi being one, also allow the situation to speak for itself. Henry Longhurst, the late British commentator, was the best at letting the story unravel before the viewers' eyes.

Now, the dynamics of the Masters has flip-flopped. Faldo is in the fairway and tied for the lead, while Floyd faces a difficult drive on the last hole: a winding dogleg right with traps left and trees right.

Faldo hits the green in regulation and two putts for par. Floyd drives into the fairway bunker, then misses the green into the right green-side bunker. With the tournament slipping away, he remains focused and unhurried. He plays a remarkable bunker shot and saves par to tie Faldo.

What have we learned watching this scene?

From Faldo: Stay in the ball game. Play shots you feel confident about. Stick to your game plan.

From Floyd: Even when the complexion of the tournament changes for the worse, stay calm and concentrated. You can still save par on a par four after hitting two bad shots. One good shot can save the day.

From here, we all know what happened. Faldo won the 1990 Masters in sudden death when Floyd's second shot found the water on hole number eleven.

It's remarkable to me how dedicated Faldo was with that game plan. With one hole to go and with the Masters title on the line, Faldo still did not "go for it" off the eighteenth tee. He stuck with his plan, and he won the tournament.

Later that year at the 1990 U.S. Open Championship, Faldo again faced the same type of situation. He was one stroke behind playing the seventy-second hole. This time, Hale Irwin was already finished and in the clubhouse. Faldo needed a birdie. The eighteenth at Medinah is 440 yards long and doglegs left. Most players hit driver here, but not Faldo. He teed with a one iron to hit into the widest section of fairway during the first three rounds.

Would he do it again, knowing that he needed birdie; knowing that a one iron would leave him a long iron to the green, while a perfectly hit drive could leave him a short iron?

Faldo doesn't hesitate. He hits the one iron and leaves himself a three iron second shot. He hits a great shot fifteen feet from the hole and lips the cup for the birdie he needed to tie.

Did Faldo use the proper strategy? Definitely. He played the tee shot with confidence. He hit the ball in the fairway. He gave himself a great chance to score birdie, by playing the hole as he planned.

Surely, some thought Faldo should have hit driver. I recalled that at least one commentator second-guessed Faldo's choice of club. But some commentators make every shot an earth-shattering all-time pressurized moment in golf. They make it seem like the tour player is feeling the greatest strain of his or her career. You need to remember that this is not always true. In fact, often the seasoned golfer relishes these moments. Often, the pro plays better, not worse.

Take Tom Kite, for example, who hit a driver off the tee on the last hole of the 1992 U.S. Open at Pebble Beach. Most people would have thought Kite was under incredible stress. Yet, in reality, he told me that he felt great. He felt extremely confident that he *would* hit the driver in the fairway. In his mind, there was no reason for him to play safe with a three wood or one iron, even though the Pacific Ocean borders the left side of the eighteenth fairway and out-of-bounds stakes border the right side.

If you recall the situation, Kite had a two-shot lead coming to the final hole of this coveted championship. Some so-called experts thought he should have played safe off the tee, to ensure a score of no worse than bogey and a win. Not Kite. He played aggressively with his best club—the driver. He hit the ball hard down the fairway, just as if he were banging balls at the driving range on a Sunday afternoon.

Did Kite feel scared or frightened? No. Despite this being his best-ever opportunity to win his first Major, he did not play safe and he did not allow himself to think about what a win would mean to his career. He stayed "in the zone." He followed his game plan.

What can you learn from this situation? First, commentators make it seem as though no one could cope. They make the hazards huge and foremost in your mind as you watch the telecast. On the other hand, the tour player diminishes the hazards. The golfer aligns his or her mind with positive images. The tour player stays in the present moment and takes a shot-by-shot approach to every round of golf. He or she doesn't change that approach on the eighteenth hole of the last round unless necessary.

I'm not saying that no one chokes or that poor decisions are not made under stress. I am saying that these great players are trained to handle tough situations. I am saying that inwardly they are not thinking what some announcers would have you believe. I am saying that you should look and learn yourself. Notice how the golfer reacts and if he or she remains calm and focused. There is an unmistakable look and attitude in a champion. To me, such a player looks in control of the situation and as if he or she had a strong sense of security via an inner determination to get the job done. The pro does not appear panicky, distracted, or out of control. Instead, he or she appears to be in total control. The top tour player gives the appearance of assurance and confidence, which certainly helps create the feeling of inward confidence and mental toughness.

What can you learn? When you're nervous or face a personally frightening golf shot, change your body language. Think of
your personal golf hero and imagine how he or she would look
under similar circumstances. Then copy that appearance.
Always try to look as though you knew what you are doing.

Do not underestimate the value of body language.
Standing proud, looking comfortable, making fluid body
movements, and staying in control have profound internal
effects. They make a big difference about how you will feel
inside. Slow your movements down, calm down, and breathe
slower. Look like a professional and you'll have much more
success.

The opposite approach to pressure situations is the golfer
who ultimately fails badly. Such a player has shallow breathing
and appears nervous, with the eyes darting in different directions. He or she might even demonstrate obvious inappro-
priate behavior.

Dysfunctional body language, outward appearance, and
inward self-talk can be changed. Copy the great competitors
such as Jack Nicklaus, who is probably the best model of all
time. Change your act. Learn from the best while watching golf
on television.

My good friend Dr. Fran Pirozzolo offers this advice on body
language:

> Stay decisive and positive in your movements, no
> matter how tough the course situation you face. If you
> see trouble, do not ignore it, but simply recognize it. If
> there is the Pacific Ocean guarding the left side of the
> fairway, it's unlikely you won't see it. However, instead
> of focusing on the water hazard, focus on your target
> and strike the ball with confidence.

Fran also says to let the word *so* be the casual connector
between the hazard and a last positive thought. For example,
"Ocean is to the left, *so* hit it hard at the center of the fairway."

If your last thought is "Don't hit the ball into the ocean,"
then your brain will picture *ocean*. And that's where the ball will
likely land!

When you see a great player like Tom Kite hit a perfect drive under pressure and avoid trouble, you can be assured that before he swung the club he had a clear, positive picture of that perfect shot run through his mind—one as clear as the picture on your television screen.

Look and learn.

TEE TIME
THE ART OF DRIVING THE BALL WITH AUTHORITY

"If you can't drive the ball, you can't play good golf."

—BEN HOGAN

"The most important club in the bag, in my opinion, is the driver."

—BYRON NELSON

These statements by two of golf's greatest players cannot be ignored.

Although a strong argument can be made that good putting is the most efficient way to lower scores, a reliable driving game seems to be a common denominator of all golf champions. You cannot underestimate the importance of driving the ball well. A successful drive off the first tee sets a positive tone for the entire round, no matter what level player you are. *Jack Nicklaus has even called it the most important shot of the day.* If you can consistently hit the ball far down the fairway, you are a skilled driver with a tremendous competitive advantage. Good driving puts you in an offensive position, whereas weak driving puts you in a defensive position.

This chapter is devoted to the unique requirements and tactics of driving. In no way, however, do I believe there is a separate driver swing. Yet I would like to share some important *setup* adjustments and *mental* adjustments that are unique to the driver swing and can greatly aid your performance off the tee. These ideas correlate with the material in Chapter 7, "The Eight-Step Swing," but they favor some parameters and preferences that were designated "acceptable" in that chapter but that I identify here as being particularly suited to better driving.

Ken Venturi's influence is evident throughout my statements and writings about the golf swing, and his approach to driving impresses me as much today as it did in the mid-1970s. During that period, I played many rounds with Venturi, which is to say, I witnessed a master shot maker one on one. Venturi's ball striking was pure genius. I roomed with Bruce Lietzke, Bill Rogers, and

John Mahaffey at the University of Houston, and I have played numerous competitive rounds with Lanny Wadkins, Tom Kite, Ben Crenshaw, Johnny Miller, and others. Although all of them were/are tremendous ball strikers, none of them could maneuver the ball with the precision of Venturi. When I played with him, away from tournament pressure, when putting did not matter, Venturi could still do absolutely anything with the golf ball, on command. Here are the best driving tips he has shared with me.

A *Use a wide base.* The best drivers place their feet wider than shoulder width apart. Past professionals who were considered premier drivers and who played from a wide

Two driving tips emphasized by Ken Venturi were assume a wide base and lower your center of gravity.

SAME, SAME, SAME

Driving, unlike any other shot in golf, allows you to eliminate most variables. Most every teeing area is dead flat, the grass on the tee is mowed low, you can tee your ball to exactly the same height every time, and you can create the angle you want by teeing up next to the left or right marker, or between them. So what you want to do on the tee is to create the "basketball free throw" mentality. That is, make every drive the same. Change nothing. Go through the same routine every time and play the same drive on every hole. Allow no variables in your thinking or your shot pattern.

base include Ben Hogan and Byron Nelson. Today, Lee Trevino, Arnold Palmer, and Bruce Lietzke depend on the same setup key. The wide base encourages a shallower swing and an elongated "flat spot" through the hitting area, which is ideal for accurate driving. The wide stance provides a low center of gravity for stability and allows a player to "pump" the feet off the ground more powerfully. If you had one chance to deliver your hardest punch and win the heavyweight crown, you would instinctively spread your feet. When a baseball slugger connects with power, it's because he or she has stepped forward and hit from a broad base.

Ⓑ *Play the ball off your left heel.* This ball position takes maximum advantage of the flat spot in your sweeping driver swing.

Ⓒ *Favor a fade.* Many fine golfers play a fade because they find it to be the ideal control shot in golf. If you're strong and have good hand-eye coordination, try it.

One of the great professional drivers of all time is Bruce Lietzke. I lived with Lietzke at the University of Houston (we also roomed together at all away tournaments and, later, on the mini Tour), and I'd like to pass on some of my observations.

Lietzke has reduced all his planning and thinking to a bare minimum. Every drive Lietzke hits is the same: he aims down the left side of every fairway. He visualizes the ball *fading* into the center of the landing area. He addresses his ball and trusts his swing. He lets go. Lietzke's "fade control" is the chief reason why he is usually the PGA Tour's best overall driver. This category combines distance and accuracy.

An average putter at best, Lietzke has been a money machine on the Tour. What's more, he rarely practices and actually plays fewer events than any Tour regular. Super talented? Yes, but Lietzke also has superior golf smarts. He eliminates the left side of every hole on every golf course he plays. This is especially beneficial in driving, because driving is what sets up good scoring possibilities.

Lietzke's driving game allows him to stay on the *offensive* at all times, especially down the stretch. If you looked up Lietzke's final-round scoring average over his career, you'll see it is one of the best ever. One major reason for his Sunday success is Lietzke's ability to drive it long and straight.

I hold up Lietzke's driving game as a model for my students to emulate. Especially in your driving, go up there with a plan, a visual picture, and a chosen shot shape. Eliminate every variable you can. Keep your plan and all your thoughts as simple as possible.

Of course, you may naturally ask, "What does Bruce Lietzke do when he comes to a hole that requires a right-to-left tee shot?" The answer is so simple, it's scary: he doesn't hit his driver. As Lietzke says, his driver "is not allowed to know it can hook the ball!"

Along with Lietzke, there have been quite a few other top performers whose driving games have been based on a controlled, powerful fade. Jack Nicklaus, Ben Hogan, Lee Trevino, and Hale Irwin all played the power fade. For aspiring players, this should be food for thought.

SWING LEFT TO SWING RIGHT

For many people, the effort to swing to a high finish or to stay behind the ball will bring the arms up high early past impact. With this arm action, the shaft tilts to a markedly vertical orientation. Even for the advanced player, this style of release needs explanation. By nature, shots hit from this position are more oblique to the target line and can stray farther left or right than the swing action would seem to indicate. Generally, though, it's a hooking topspin sort of action that is imparted.

The swing thought that will prevent this error is "low arms through impact." I ask my advanced students to keep both arms down past impact and underneath the shoulders all the way to the waist-high position. To do this, keep the horizontal lines of the body more level through the swing. As the downswing begins, the right shoulder drops and begins to rotate forward. Even though you know it will lower, think "level." The swing-left-low, arms-on-plane follow-through requires most players to feel a high right side.

Another productive thought can be to pull the left arm and the golf club consciously leftward with center. This is done with a rock-solid left wrist with no breakdown; there is a feeling of the back of the left wrist and the left arm staying with the rotation of the body and *pulling left*. Again, this is a great antihook image, one that has worked well for tour player Bill Britton. We've employed it to help him straighten out his shots immensely.

The basic dynamics of this left-sided pulling motion can be encapsulated in the following manner: stand up near a wall, with your right shoulder and right side several feet away, and extend your left arm as if you were about to shake hands using your left hand. Your left arm is bent at the elbow and the palm of your left hand is open. Your left palm will directly face the wall. Make sure you feel a bend in that left elbow and that you feel a strong *connectedness* that comes out of your left shoulder and left pectoral region, extending almost all the way down to the elbow. Now shut your hand fairly tightly as though you have just grasped the end of a chain that you are attempting to pull out of the wall. To pull the chain free you would use your whole body. Your left arm would stay connected to the rotation of the body and you'd jerk that chain out of the wall in a "level left" movement. This has been a tremendous teaching thought for me, which I sometimes extend to a feeling of the left shoulder staying down through the shot.

Another positive, effective image I have used with Britton is the Charlie Sifford swing, in which Sifford swings the arms underneath his trademark cigar. Sifford, of course, was a cigar smoker, and anyone who has seen him play golf would notice a very high right side, a low left side, and a very forward motion going through the ball. Sifford has been one of the great straight-ball hitters and drivers of all time.

I had the opportunity to play with Sifford and found he was also a particularly great wind player. The trajectory of his ball was down, because he moved his body with such a level turn, keyed by his high right side. This is a tremendous way to play golf, because it has the appearance of a "comeover," but it produces a beautiful, straight golf shot. This is the swing feeling that Britton adopted to win the 1989 Centel Classic. He felt as though he were staying under the cigar and going left through the golf shot with a low finish or, you might say, a "high right side."

Yet another swing key you can work on to groove a hookproof swing is to allow your *right arm* to go across your chest as the clubhead moves through the ball. If you do this correctly, your hands will feel as if they were left of your right shoulder through impact, almost in a *crossing motion*. Once again, this tip is for golfers who stay behind the ball too long and swing the club out to the right too much. They have experienced overkill on the *inside-out motion*. I see many lower-handicap players who have worked hard to achieve the inside-out swing and as a result have lost the chance to play really good golf. They are destined to hook the ball the rest of their golfing life unless they can correct their swing path problem.

In working extensively with Tom Kite throughout 1992, this hookproof swing-left concept was the single greatest change he made. I believe it increased Kite's accuracy through the bag and definitely helped him drive the ball much farther.

A Little Help from My Friends

A Driving Tip from Al Mengert

The first golf lessons I ever took were in Seattle in 1966, from Al Mengert, who had worked under Claude Harmon at Winged Foot and Tommy Armour in Boca Raton. Mengert showed me that from the tee the fairway was actually a *three-lane highway.*

If you play a draw, you should aim down the right lane and plan to land the ball on the center lane (middle of fairway). If you hit it straight, you end up in the right lane—the right side of the fairway, which is fine. If you hit your planned shot, you are dead center: "Position A." If you hit too much draw, chances are you will still end up in the left lane of the fairway. (Never aim a drive so that a straight ball will go into trouble.) This "driver's education lesson" will allow you to use the *whole fairway* and increase your chances of staying on the short grass.

A Driving Tip from Jackie Burke

When I played on the golf team at the University of Houston, we had the opportunity to play with and learn from Jackie Burke—one of golf's finest thinkers who won both the Masters and PGA Championships. Burke didn't just suggest to us that we "let go with the driver," he preached it nonstop! He found the idea of guiding or steering your drives totally repugnant. "Let go. Give up control. Abandonment." These are the ideas he adhered to in regard to driving. To be great, he told us, "you must have some *recklessness* to your swing."

The best visual image he offered was this: "Imagine you are trying to drive the ball into the Atlantic Ocean. There is no way to miss. You could hit it anywhere. So swing freely." He reasoned that with no interfering thoughts we would find ourselves hitting solid drives virtually on a string.

This single thought has helped me get through some tremendously stressful situations in decent fashion. I highly recommend this *let go* mentality whenever the going gets particularly tough.

Drills to Improve Your Driving

1. *Train Your Right Side*
   Practice a natural side-arm tossing motion with your right arm. Practice the correct positions in the Eight Steps by swinging a club with your right hand and arm only.
2. *Play Tee-ball Golf*
   When you can, play nine holes alone. Hit ten drives off each tee, then go to the next hole. Assuming the nine has two par-three holes, you will be hitting seventy driver shots to actual landing areas of regulation holes. Keep track of the number of fairways you hit.
3. *Drag the Clubhead*
   Gardner Dickinson, a legendary player and teacher, devised a drill that helps you swing in such a way that

the clubhead approaches the ball on a shallower angle, ensuring solid contact. For good players, this drill produces the feeling of taking the hands out of the swing.

Address an imaginary ball and take your normal stance, but set the clubhead down even with your right foot. Make sure the clubhead is inside the target line and the clubface is open. Now drag the clubhead forward through the imaginary ball, making a conscious effort to close the clubface—to square the toe through impact. On the follow-through, the toe of the clubface should point skyward. Continue through to a full, balanced finish, extending your right arm while the left arm folds at the elbow. This will give you the sensation of the no-hands release and shallower angle of approach through impact and into the finish position.

Swinging with your right hand only will improve your driving skills.

④ *Sweep the Ball Drill*

This has been a lifesaver drill I've used for good players who experience a severe driving slump; it teaches many of the fundamentals seen in great drivers. It is performed with a fairway wood that features four or five wood loft, a shallow face, and a smaller-profile clubhead. Because the point of the drill is to pick the ball cleanly off the tee with a sweeping swing, this type of club is ideal. That's because any swings delivered along a steep swing path will produce an extra-high "skied" shot; letting you know instantly that your technique was incorrect.

To do the drill, tee the ball one inch off the ground. Check all your alignments and check your posture as you address the ball. Unify your hands at address, by establishing a secure grip that still allows mobility in the wrists. Grip slightly tighter in the last three fingers of the left hand. Now swing back with what feels like a half-backswing, at about 60 percent of full force. Because the club and arms never get high in the backswing, you cannot swing along a steep incline.

Initiate the change of direction from backswing to forward swing *from the ground up*. The clubhead will be only about waist high in the backswing as you initiate the forward motion. Feel your feet, knees, and hips shift laterally. This lateral movement should occur before the clubhead has completed its backward arc. Once it's triggered, the clubshaft will fall into the slot (i.e., approach the ball from an inside and shallow "attack track"), wrist cock will increase, the right elbow will start down toward the ball, the width of the swing will narrow dramatically from the backswing to the forward swing, and you will sense an *out-to-in* or *wide-to-narrow action*.

As you swing through the ball fully, make a "no-hands" release and keep your left wrist solid. Allow your left elbow to fold after impact and your right arm to elongate.

If you made no effort to swing with your hands, you'll feel the club sweeping powerfully through the ball, with the clubface staying on the clubface longer at impact. You'll also feel your hands and arms coming up in front of your chest, which is a good sign. It is truly an awesome feeling to experience.

The shot you will hit is a low, line-drive draw; the draw coming not from flipping the hands but instead from "firing" your entire right side. One final point to check on your no hands back-and-through swing: look for the toe of the club to be up on both sides of the swing.

Remember: It's a mini-swing drill with the purpose being to deliver a shallow arc. The small swing done correctly will give you incredible distance—much more than expected.

⑤ *Hit Drives between Flagpoles*

On the range, pick out a thirty-yard-wide landing area, then hit drives into the gap between two real or imaginary flagpoles. Keep track of your success rate whenever you do this. I recommend that you hit thirty drives, keeping track of how many fairways you hit.

Jim McLean's Tip Sheet for Good Driving

On the tee, you should

- Use a driver that is aesthetically pleasing to the eye and features the correct loft, lie, and shaft flex for *you*.
- Adhere to a confident preshot routine.
- Love the challenge of driving the ball powerfully and accurately.
- Think positively.
- Play a shot.
- Relax your grip pressure when you set up.
- Soften your arms and keep your wrists flexible at address.
- Feel and sense the center of your body initiating the swing.
- Connect your arm swing to the rotation of your body.
- Employ good footwork.
- Stay level during the swing.
- Strive for solid contact and center hits.
- Make your right shoulder, right hip, and right knee finish past the centerline of your body that is first established at address.
- Drive the ball through an imaginary window, positioned ten feet out in front of you, along the target line.

Great drivers:

- Visualize the optimum shot. Don't freeze over the ball; stay in motion before pulling the trigger.
- Let go.
- Have two pivot points (the two legs) in their swings.
- Have some lateral motion in their swings.
- Have a shallow angle of attack.
- Have a long flat spot in their swings.
- Hit past the ball.
- Go to a full finish position.
- Have an athletic motion.
- Swing within themselves.
- Have extra power in reserve.

PLAYING TO YOUR POTENTIAL
THE SECRET IS ACCURATE SELF-EVALUATION

How many golfers do you know whose swings are far short of classic? Who don't get much distance on their drives? Who play a slice with every club but the short irons? And who, despite these shortcomings, post impressive scores and often win the "Nassau bet"? These are the golfers who know themselves and know their games, who play within themselves and are good course managers. As John Wooden (the wizard of UCLA) once said, "Don't let what you cannot do interfere with what you can do."

To make sure we distribute the satisfaction these golfers feel more widely among the population, teachers must begin emphasizing course management so that students understand that management skills depend on how well they know themselves and their game and how well they translate this knowledge into a sound plan by which to play each hole.

When sports psychology experts like Dick Coop, Bob Rotella, Fran Pirozzolo, and Chuck Hogan discuss the mental side of golf, they never stray far from the principle of *self-knowledge*. Of all games, golf exposes fraud and self-delusion most efficiently. There is no other sport besides perhaps the high jump or pole vault in which, before we play, it is so obvious what we are trying to do. In effect, we golfers call our shots every time we come to bat. If we can point to the center field bleachers (by selecting our three wood trying to reach a lakeside par five from 240 yards) then hit the ball there, hurrah for us. Likewise, if we can plan the golf equivalent of a walk, a hit-and-run single, and a squeeze bunt, and still make birdie, we've succeeded just as well. If you are not in touch with your own ability and your own golf psyche, your competitors will know soon enough that—whatever kind of player you are—you've got a lousy manager in *your* dugout.

In the past few years, CBS's Gary McCord and other TV golf announcers have described many a successful golf shot by calling it a "good play." This phrase has always been appropriate to sports in which the athlete must react to a situation, such as when a shortstop charges a slow roller and throws home or a point guard hits the open player underneath for a layup. But in golf, with a ball and a target that don't move, does it make sense to say, "good play"? The answer is yes, absolutely. The key is not whether things are moving or standing still, it's whether or not there are options and choices. Like the shortstop and the point guard, the golfer has options. He or she has more time to think but also has a greater number of options, on most shots. When tour players assess the lie, the competition's standing, the score they need to make, and the strengths and weaknesses of their game, they are reacting to a situation. If they read the situation improperly, they can hit what you'd have to call a good shot and still be in trouble. When they devise a plan—from club selection, to swing technique, to the shape of the shot—and go on to execute it, the two words they are truly hoping to hear from the caddie are *good play*.

Most of us make good plays when we are at peace with ourselves and feel an inward calm. Here are two proven ways to achieve a golf state of mind that will enhance your performance.

● *Assess the game you've brought to the course that day.* Once you take an honest account of the current state of your golf skills, you are ready to establish a game plan based on shots you are comfortable executing, as opposed to shots you can only hope to hit. For each hole, you should have a plan based on shots that you are at least 50 percent chance for success.

- *Commit yourself to target golf.* Good course management is a matter of *targets and plans.* From the first swing on the first tee until the final putt on hole number eighteen, you will do nothing but define your targets and plan realistic ways to reach them. Obviously, no plan works perfectly; that's why it's called a plan. There will almost always be shots that stray from the plan and miss the target by a substantial margin. When this happens, you play a recovery shot that permits you to get back to your game plan as soon as possible. The other option is mentally to beat yourself up for failing to execute, and that's the classic mental *Death Move.* Even on recovery shots, you are still dealing with a target and a plan—you hope a very reasonable one. Dr. Pirozzolo says to commit 100 percent to every shot, and then use 80 percent effort to execute the shot. You do not get a peak performance by overtrying. Keep something in reserve. This will help you relax and execute under pressure.

To be aware of targets throughout your round of golf—as opposed to being totally preoccupied with hitting the ball—is a big step for a golfer. It's the difference between playing golf and spending eighteen holes trying to make golf swings. Always ask yourself, "What am I trying to do?" Then proceed with your plan by employing a swing that represents 80 percent physical effort but 100 percent mental commitment. Any time a golfer of reasonable skill sets up over a shot that requires a mere half swing and almost whiffs the shot—chunking it a few feet forward or skulling it twice the intended distance, the problem was in the *plan.* His or her conscious mind put in a call for a swing that was, in most cases, either too strong or too weak. On the downswing, the unconscious mind realized the problem and hit the panic button. The original plan was aborted, and what happened then is the golf equivalent of football's broken play. As in football, a broken play in golf, or what we call a "good miss," can sometimes work out well. It's a mistake to blame the Execution Department for a major error made by the Planning Department. On your next shot, the plan may be sound, but having lost some confidence in your ability to make a swing, you may not execute it.

Basic Tips for Good Course Management

- *Stay Focused.* Pay attention to what must be accomplished in the present. Tune out your three-putt on the last hole (the past). Forget the tough par-five next hole (the future). The only important shot in the entire round is the present shot, the one you have to hit next.
- *Have Confidence.* The attitude you must walk around with is one that has you believing you will successfully hit every shot as long as you stay focused. If you are playing within your capabilities, there is no reason to doubt your ability to execute the plan and reach the target.
- *Relax.* Trying to make things happen, rather than staying relaxed and *letting them happen*, is the great builder of tension. Tension usually destroys the naturalness of your golf swing. If you feel tension building, concentrate on keeping your hands and arms soft—especially at address but all throughout the swing as well. Keep the hands and arms soft, and you dramatically increase your odds of making a good swing. Perhaps the most important words in golf are *Let Go* or *Let It Happen*. It's okay to be nervous, even scared, at times. However, you can and you must find a way to relax your hands and arms.
- *Hit through the Window.* Any time a golfer conducts a complete analysis of the shot that must be played, there is the possibility that he or she eventually begins seeing everything that could go wrong. In a pressure situation, you may be wise to assess your situation fairly quickly, keeping most of your preshot focus on the good, smooth swing you want to make. Stand behind your ball, then pick an aiming point about ten feet ahead of the ball that

is a suspended window at the height you desire. This window image will reduce your peripheral sight and help you concentrate on the swing. Now just hit the ball through the window. Even if it is not a perfect shot, the ball will likely start on line. If there were a window out in front of you on every shot, you would accelerate the club through the ball at good speed and hit many more good shots per round. Again, avoid taking too much time analyzing; avoid all thoughts of where not to hit the ball.

● *"If I Don't Hit a Good Shot—So What."* Let's face it, many golfers put far too much pressure on themselves. Trying for perfection can be dangerous. No one is perfect, and golf will always be a game of misses. Sometimes not trying is a big tension reliever. An example could be on a crucial four-foot putt. Instead of thinking, "I must hole this putt," try telling yourself, "If I don't hole this putt, so what." No one will put you in front of a firing squad. You'll be surprised how many putts you will make. Try this same strategy in any other pressure-filled shot-making situation.

KEEPING SCORE

There is an alternative approach to score keeping that for some of my students has changed their entire outlook on playing a round of golf. Instead of reporting the results of each hole in strict numerical terms, this kind of score keeping gives the shot-by-shot record of a given round. It lists fairways hit, greens hit in regulation, bunker saves, total number of putts, etc. You can play a point game for each fairway hit and each green hit in regulation. Try to achieve a target score. This takes you mind off the score.

Improvement in these various aspects of golf is the true indication of progress, and defining your day of golf in this way also makes you a much better course manager. When golfers concentrate on these *shot-by-shot* challenges, they stop putting themselves down for the few bad shots they hit. Over a period of time, the alternative scorecards provide an excellent readout of strengths and weaknesses, which means practice time can be budgeted all the more effectively.

SUMMARY

Course management is an interesting and critically important part of your golf game. Choosing targets and devising plans for each shot is a constant mental—and emotional—challenge that truly requires self-knowledge and a shrewd judgment of talent—your own talent, that is. When you get to the point at which you are playing smart golf—doing all the little things that make the difference between shooting one hundred or eighty-eight, eighty-six or seventy-eight, seventy-four or sixty-eight, losing a match or winning it—you will be enjoying this game in the best way possible.

Unfortunately, the majority of golfers never fully recognize the importance of course management. Even after reading an entire book about course management, many golfers will go out on the course and get overwhelmed by all the strategy options. For many, also, the discipline required for all the preshot details is too much to handle. For those who build up their mental technique and really learn to think their way around the golf course, the rewards include not just well-played golf but a larger understanding of themselves and the world around them.

TEACHER TALK
WHAT TO EXPECT FROM A QUALITY GOLF INSTRUCTOR

Golf instructors are almost unanimous in saying, "Students come in all different skill levels and interest levels, so you can't teach the same swing to everyone. That's why I would never teach only one method or any one system."

While I agree that people are different and their swings naturally differ, I also believe that a good instructor has a systematic approach to teaching and is extremely consistent in what he or she espouses. All good teachers have fundamental ideas that they stick with. Bad teachers dramatically change their philosophies either from year to year, month to month, week to week, or day to day!

Consistency is an important attribute in an instructor. What you want is a teacher whose grasp of the fundamentals is complete, who has a sharp eye for your swing problems, and in turn has the patience to spoon-feed you ideas and information at appropriate intervals. Most of all, you want a teacher who can tell you the things you *cannot* do as well as what you *must* do. If this sounds like a negative approach, I find it has made my instruction more definitive and less confining for the student. Even when I describe a flaw in a pupil's swing (by using the unnerving term *Death Move*), he or she has no need to despair. I tell my students that parameters exist, they have options, and there is leeway in terms of what will work. But, at the edge of those parameters lies Death Valley—all the off-limits swing positions from which there is virtually no escape.

A positive attitude is a must for good teaching, but negative commentary also plays its role. In fact, it can work wonders. Making every comment positive and upbeat is, frankly, confining, eventually confusing, and counterproductive. Some-times you'll need to hear the words *This has got to stop.*

In this age of specialization, even golf professionals are tracking in narrower skill areas and letting go of the idea that they can master every skill category in the profession. Obviously, my choice was to concentrate on teaching, but as director of golf at a high-profile country club, my responsibilities to the membership have been demanding and varied. To make sure all these areas were covered in a completely satisfactory manner, I assembled a staff that included people with expertise in the entire operation.

One of the things you look for in a teacher is that *he or she spends a lot of time teaching.* Without a strong support team and the ability to supervise and delegate, the professional cannot concentrate adequately on teaching. An instructor who teaches a heavy schedule of lessons usually has solid ideas and the ability to communicate them. This is not an absolute corollary, but at the very least it is one significant clue.

Having the title "golf professional" does not automatically make someone a great golf instructor any more than the title "professor" makes someone a great educator. From our days in high school and college we all know that some instructors were better than others, even though they taught from the same books and had the same opportunities. In point of fact, some professors were infinitely better than others. Here, in brief, are the additional characteristics I feel a top-quality golf instructor will display:

- *Commitment to becoming the best.* It's easy for teachers to say they strive for teaching excellence, but when they start counting up the hours of work, the money that must be invested, and the opportunities that must be sought out, they realize the commitment becomes difficult to fulfill. Pick a teacher who is truly committed.
- *Long roster of success stories.* A teacher's best sales tool is his or her legion of satisfied students. The two very best questions: "Do this teacher's students get better?" and "Who are they?"
- *Total understanding of the complete game.* There is more to teaching golf than the full swing. A top-notch instructor

The throwing action of a baseball pitcher will help you understand the basic law of human motion that prevails in a powerful golf swing.

must also teach putting, chipping, bunker play, course management, club fitting, and the many other little areas students want help in. This versatility only comes through tremendous effort, preparation, and training.

● *Clear understanding of the basic swing motion.* A "quality" teacher must understand the undeniable law of human motion, as well as the basic physics of the swing itself. This law refers to a certain sequence of movements that prevails in most throwing motions, such as pitching a baseball, throwing a football, or launching a javelin.

● *Multiple ways to make the point.* Command of terminology and a creative golf vocabulary are a must for the versatile teacher. A top instructor must be able to communicate to golfers who play at all levels.

● *Confidence and interest.* Your golf instructor has to care about your progress and has to convince you of your potential. If a golf professional has to force these feelings, the student will sense it immediately.

- *A good eye and good video*. I believe so firmly in the value of video I can't imagine any serious teacher not using it. I know, from having worked with many instructors, that there are some tremendous veterans who do very well without video. The answer must be that they have extremely sharp eyes for what happens in the swing and great coaching skills. I feel my own acuity for spotting flaws and noticing small increments of progress has only been enhanced by looking at so much slow-motion, stop-action videotape of the swing. At the very least, it confirms to both me and the student that my observation was correct. The top instructor makes an accurate diagnosis time after time.
- *An ability to demonstrate*. Although not mandatory, it's awfully nice to see the teacher "do it himself or herself." This demonstration of the proper technique stimulates the student and speeds the learning process.

Fine instructors in all professions don't all do things the same way. These remarks of mine are intended to put across some of the notable attributes of an effective teacher of golf. Selecting the person who can help you improve the most will take some effort, but I promise you it will be worth your research time to find that top-quality teacher who can coach you to discover all aspects of the game of golf.

WHAT I EXPECT FROM A QUALITY STUDENT

Having been lucky enough to work with many top tour pros, I would like to give you some of my observations. I'll start with a story about the greatest student, learner, and practicer since Ben Hogan—Tom Kite.

At Doral, in 1992, I was working very hard with Kite on several difficult swing changes. Knowing Kite, I told him exactly what I thought about the status of his technique. That is exactly what he always wants from me. He determined that what I told him was correct, so we set about making the changes on Tuesday of tournament week.

Now, understand that when Kite works on something he puts 100 percent effort into it. We made a dramatic change in his follow-through, which was geared to altering his swing path through impact. We taped it, reviewed it, retaped, reviewed again, and again, and again.

All too soon, it was Thursday, tournament time. One of my instructors followed Kite on the first three holes that morning and it wasn't pretty. He came back and told me that Tom had hit the worst snap hook ever on hole number three into a lake about 150 yards off the tee—and this came after a five, five start. Needless to say, my heart sank. Could I have ruined Kite? Was he on his way to his highest score of the year?

About four hours later Kite walked onto the tee at the Doral Learning Center, and I went over to meet him. Not knowing what he shot, I simply asked him (with my heart in my throat). Thankfully, it was seventy-three. Next, I asked him how he hit the ball. Kite said he had started weak but had hit some excellent shots. I then said, "I heard about the drive on number three—did you just forget about what we were working on after that and get back to something you could play with to get it around for today?"

I was a little taken back by Kite's response which was, "What do you mean, Jim?"

So I had to start over. "Well, did you go back to some different ideas?"

Tom looked at me as if I were crazy. He said forcefully, "Jim, I made a few bad swings out there, but the thought of changing never occurred to me. I *know* we are working on the right things. I don't care how I hit it today—I'm going to make the corrections necessary for the future."

That was the end of the conversation. We went right back to working on *the same things*.

Incidentally on Sunday, the last round, Tom hit every fairway with his driver and all eighteen greens in regulation. He came down to the Learning Center all pumped up and told me it was the best ball-striking round he had experienced in more than a year. He finished sixty-five, sixty-nine on the weekend, for a sixth-place finish. One month later he won at Atlanta and soon after captured the U.S. Open at Pebble Beach.

One more telling story. A week after watching Nick Faldo practice at our range at the Doral Learning Center, I drove over to Weston Hills (site of the 1993 Honda Classic) to work with several players.

On the range was Faldo, so I took the opportunity to watch him practice. This time he was with his coach, David Lead-better, and several other professionals. Faldo was hitting driver after driver all pretty tasty. Periodically, Faldo would talk with Leadbetter or make several practice motions. For one particular drive, he spent five minutes or so doing a simple drill. Then he addressed the ball and hit another great-looking drive; only this one flew ten yards farther. Faldo looked over at the group and smiled broadly. Then, to my surprise, he pumped his fist wildly and went into a little jig. Obviously, he was extremely pleased by that last drive; I mean really happy!

The thought occurred to me; here was the number one player in the world as excited about a great practice-range drive as any young teenager might be smoking a long, straight tee shot. Maybe more excited!

There is a big lesson here. *Appreciate the brilliant shots you hit. Give yourself credit. Remember your good shots and make them important—even on the practice tee.*

Most golfers do just the opposite. They make a big deal about the bad shots, throwing clubs or criticizing themselves unmercifully. Don't you. Take a lesson from the world's greatest students.

Faldo and Kite play golf because they love it. To them it is *art.* They paint pictures with their clubs. Neither one can wait for the next day of golf.

Great students love the game.

TOM KITE'S SUPER SWING

STEP FIVE: Move Down to the Ball

STEP SIX: Impact